W9-CEA-387

Principles of
Law Enforcement
Report Writing

Gino Arcaro
Niagara College

McGraw-Hill Ryerson Limited
Toronto   Montreal   New York   Auckland   Bogotá   Caracas
Lisbon   London   Madrid   Mexico   Milan   New Delhi
San Juan   Singapore   Sydney   Tokyo

McGraw-Hill
Ryerson Limited
A Subsidiary of The McGraw-Hill Companies

PRINCIPLES OF LAW ENFORCEMENT REPORT WRITING

ISBN: 0-07-552773-1

1 2 3 4 5 6 7 8 9 10 W 6 5 4 3 2 1 0 9 8 7

Printed and bound in Canada

Care has been taken to trace ownership of copyright material contained in this text. The publisher will gladly take any information that will enable them to rectify any reference or credit in subsequent editions.

Sponsoring Editor: Gord Muschett
Developmental Editor: Marianne Minaker
Production Co-ordinator: Nicla Dattolico
Cover Design: Dianna Little
Cover Illustration: Steffon Sepa
Printing & Binding: Webcom

Canadian Cataloguing in Publication Data

Arcaro, Gino, 1957-
    Principles of law enforcement report writing

ISBN 0-07-552773-1

1. Police reports.   I. Title.

HV8073.A7317 1996   808'.066363   C96-932101-5

Preface

A considerable potential for career advancement exists in policing. After gaining experience in the patrol branch, officers may specialize in other units including criminal investigation, narcotics investigation, traffic investigation and the identification branch.

Although several factors contribute to a police officer's career advancement, proficient report writing skills are crucial.

The wide variety of reports that officers must write requires a thorough understanding of *the general principles* that report writing is based on.

I encourage teachers and students to use this book for police report writing classes. The book contains general principles that may be used when writing any type of report and it provides an opportunity to learn a practical system to develop and master report writing skills. Additionally, the training material is the product of a former police officer's experience, creating a valuable perspective to the subject of police report writing.

Robert Sauder
Divisional Inspector
Niagara Regional Police

About the Author

Gino Arcaro B.Sc., is a professor in the Law and Security Administration Program at Niagara College of Applied Arts and Technology, Welland, Ontario. Previously, he was a police officer with the Niagara Regional Police Force for 15 years, of which 6 were in the Criminal Investigation Branch.

Additionally, he is a frequent guest lecturer in Criminology classes at Brock University and is the Case Law & Legal Editor for BLUE LINE MAGAZINE.

Gino teaches several policing courses including, Criminal Investigation & Forensic Science, Police Patrol Principles, Rules of Evidence, Criminal Code, Highway Traffic Act ,Impaired Driving and Report Writing.

He has written two books; "Criminal Investigation: Forming Reasonable Grounds" and "Impaired Driving: Forming Reasonable Grounds".

Gino is head football coach of Hill Park High School in Hamilton, Ontario.

Table of Contents

Chapter 1 - Introduction

Report Writing and the Law Enforcement Career 1

General Philosophy 3

Types of Reports 4

Chapter 2 - General Principles

Principles of Report Writing 5

Chapter 3 - General Occurrence Report

Principles and Procedures 8

Cover Page 9

Narrative 9

    Introduction (first phase) 10

    Events Before the Offence (second phase) 12

    Events During the Offence (third phase) 13

    Events After the Offence (fourth phase) 17

Examples: Break and Enter 15

    Assault 20

    Missing Person 21

Chapter 4 - Supplementary Report

Example 23

Chapter 5 - Arrest Report

Definition: Arrest 24

           Detention 24

Example: Impaired Driving 25

Chapter 6 - Witness Statement

Purpose 26

General Principles 26

Procedure 26

Examples: Break and Enter 28

           Domestic Assault 29

Chapter 7 - Crown Brief

Principles 33
Cover Page 34
Introduction 34
Witness List 34
Summary 35
Witness Statements 37
    Example: Crown Brief .... 38 - 44

Chapter 8 - Notebook

General Format 46
General Principles 47
Apply General Principles 48
    Example: Notebook 49
Recording the Interrogation 49
    Example: Notebook 51

Chapter 9 - Private Policing/Security Reports

Notebooks 52
Reports 52
Witness Statements 53
Cover Page 54
    Example: Cover Page 54
Format for G.O.R. 55
    Example: Arrest Report - Theft under $5000.00 55
Witness Statement 56
Arrest Report - Mischief under $5000.00 57
Witness Statement 57

Appendix

Glossary of Terms 59
Words commonly used in Report Writing 59

1

Introduction

Report Writing and the
Law Enforcement Career

June Doe will say:

I am forty-five years of age. I live at 10 King Street, Apt. 6 with my husband Ward. I am employed as a court clerk for Provincial Court - Family Division. On November 6, 1977, I was at home with my husband. We were watching TV. At about 9:00 p.m., I heard people screaming in the hallway of our floor. I heard a voice say, "Move out of here. Go back to where you came from." Then someone started banging on the door. I heard more yelling, such as, "Did you hear me? Move out, go back to your own country." I heard him turning the door knob trying to get into the apartment. I feared for my safety as well as my husband's. We had been living in fear for about one month. We've been threatened to move and we've had damage caused to our car. The people in the apartment across the hall have been harassing and threatening us for the past month. I called the police and officers arrived within minutes. I spoke to an officer in the doorway of my apartment and I reported this incident to him. The other officer was speaking to the people in the apartment across from ours. The tenant, Eddie, started threatening us and the officer arrested him.

signed, June Doe
9:30 p.m. Nov. 6, 1977

A uniform patrol officer was the arresting officer and the author of the above statement. June had dictated the statement to him at 10 King Street. The facts were recorded *verbatim* from June. Eddie was arrested and charged with "Attempt Break and Enter."

The witness statement above is horrible. It's content is severely deficient, vague and lacking specific details. One of the reasons was that the statement was recorded verbatim, causing a lack of structure. The accompanying general occurrence report and arrest report were just as awful, if not worse. I was the uniform patrol officer who wrote these reports, early in my police career, after having been told repeatedly about the importance of report writing. I thought the reports were adequate when I wrote them. However, the immediate criticism from various superiors taught me valuable lessons, ones that I never forgot.

The reports were re-written and the deficiencies corrected. Actually, the revisions were made easily. The information had been obtained during the investigation, but, the proper *principles of report writing* had not been applied when completing the reports. In other words, *the poor quality of these reports was completely avoidable.*

Consequences of Poor Report Writing Skills

Although I was aware of the importance of report writing, it took a bad experience to heighten my awareness and teach me lessons that endured throughout my policing career. I learned that poor report writing skills have serious consequences, including:

- causing others to believe that the author of the report lacks legal knowledge. Reports directly reflect the writer's knowledge of law. The content demonstrates whether the writer fully understands what facts are relevant to prove a specific offence. Inferior reports suggest that the writer does not know the elements that compose an offence.

- creating a perception that the writer is lazy. Experienced officers understand the need for thorough, accurate reports. When an inferior report is read by an experienced officer, the reader often assumes that the writer is too lazy to write a high-quality report.

- causing neglect or duplicity during an investigation. For example, a uniform patrol officer receives a report from a victim, of a criminal offence which is relevant to a previously reported offence. The report is assigned to a detective to continue the investigation. An inferior report may:

i) cause the detective to re-interview the victim. The victim will certainly wonder why the investigation is being repeated and may conclude that the initial patrol officer was not competent; or

ii) the detective may assume that the lack of information is **not** due to the initial officer's inadequate writing skills and that the information is simply not known. This neglect may result in an unsuccessful investigation, thereby permitting the offender to remain undetected and able to commit additional offences.

Why is Report Writing significant in a Police Career?

Advancement into the Detective Office, Drug Enforcement Units and other specialized branches is a common goal of many Police Officers. Students often ask how advancement can be accomplished. Many factors are considered, including routine daily performance. However, a critical factor is *consistent demonstration of high quality report writing.* For example, when a vacancy exists in the Detective Office, members of that branch are asked for their opinion of which Uniform Officers may qualify for the position. Commonly, recommendations are made based on the officer's consistent report writing excellence. The recommendation may simply be, "he/she writes good reports." This simple evaluation means that the evaluator believes that the Uniform Officer has displayed all the qualities necessary to advance to the Detective Office. How is the evaluation made? By reading the daily reports submitted by the Uniform Officer. This method of evaluation increases in significance in Police Services with a large number of members. In such cases, it is difficult to know each member individually. Usually, an officer's report is the primary method of allowing Supervisors and members of specialized branches to gain familiarity with him or her.

Demonstrate Personal Excellence

Distinguishing oneself is crucial to a successful career. How can you distinguish yourself as being above average and demonstrate your personal excellence to others who do not see you in action on a daily basis? The answer is simple: high quality and large volume of reports. Get involved in investigations. Be active. Submit as many reports as possible. Allow others to see your name on reports. Then, develop your writing skills to a degree that will cause others to be impressed with your knowledge, thoroughness and commitment. A solid reputation is built in this manner.

Conversely, inferior reports create a poor reputation, and reputations are hard to change.

Communication Skills

Communication represents a vital skill in police work. Police officers are constantly required to convey their thoughts to solve a multitude of problems that vary considerably in nature.

Communication skills are divided into two categories:
- verbal
- written

Verbal skills are used by officers *during the actual problem-solving process*, such as:
- witness interviews
- suspect interrogation
- dispute resolution (e.g., domestics)

These processes require skills, to verbally convey thoughts for the purpose of obtaining information and successfully resolving specific disputes and problems. Commonly, verbal skills are perceived as being the only ones that police officers utilize. They are directly associated with actual police work because they are more visible and receive greater attention and publicity than written skills. Prospective police candidates often are unaware of the hours spent by officers documenting the activities during daily duties.

Written skills are used by officers to record and communicate facts and circumstances that occurred during a specific incident in the past. Report writing composes a large percentage of police duties, a fact often forgotten because it is an activity that is not visible to the public and is not glamorized as are other aspects of police work. Report writing skills significantly impact investigations and officers' personal careers. Essentially, the quantity of required writing may qualify officers, to a degree, as being professional writers. Therefore, a goal of every police officer should be to achieve report writing mastery.

Like any skill, achieving mastery of police report writing requires combining learned principles and procedures with repeated practical experience.

Proper principles and procedures will allow comprehensive reports to be written about incidents that *vary widely in nature*. Additionally, they will overcome other obstacles; officers commonly have *limited time* to write and cannot always write in conventional office settings. General writing guidelines may increase the ability to write effectively within *time constraints* and in *non-conventional writing environments (i.e., inside a police vehicle)*.

Mastery of police report writing requires an additional element - *a compatible attitude* toward writing. A negative attitude often develops when report writing is perceived as an insignificant burden in police work. In order to excel, a perception must be developed and maintained that report writing mastery is a goal that officers must achieve and that it is a crucial factor in successful law enforcement and personal careers.

General Philosophy

1. Police reports are a means of *communication* between members of the criminal justice system. Information is conveyed by the following networks:
   - (i) from uniform patrol officer to investigator (criminal investigation branch)
   - (ii) from police to Crown Attorney
   - (iii) from Crown Attorney to accused: (to fulfill *disclosure* requirements as guaranteed under section 7 Charter)
   - (iv) from Crown Attorney to trial judge: (read in court when accused enters a guilty plea).
   - (v) from police to witnesses: (to refresh memory)
   - (vi) by an officer to him/herself: (to refresh memory)
2. The success of investigations is largely reliant upon the *thoroughness*, *relevancy* and *accuracy* of the information written in reports.

3.   A successful report eliminates neglect or duplicity during investigations.
4.   A successful report explains the *reasonable grounds* that justified certain actions,
- arrest
- laying a charge
- searching a person or place
- seizing evidence
- use of force
5.   The level of report writing skills reflects the degree of an officer's competency. An officer's knowledge of law and his/her investigative talents are revealed by written reports. Thorough reports composed of *relevant* and *accurate* information indicates that the officer is knowledgeable about the pertinent legal and investigative issues of the specific incident.
6.   Report writing skills significantly contribute to opinions formed by other members of the police organization. Consistent, high quality reports indicate a strong work ethic and are a prevalent factor used to select officers for advancement into investigative branches.

Types of Reports

1.   GENERAL OCCURRENCE REPORT (G.O.R.):
- the *initial* report of an incident made by a complainant/victim to police.
- composed of a cover page and supplementary reports.
2.   SUPPLEMENTARY REPORTS (follow-up reports):
- the *narrative* portion of the G.O.R. is written on supplementary reports. It includes the details of the initial report and all the circumstances of the subsequent investigation.
3.   ARREST REPORT:
- describes the circumstances of any occurrence where a person is arrested or detained (by definition), regardless if a charge is laid or if the offender is released unconditionally (no charges laid).
4.   WITNESS STATEMENTS:
- formal, written record of witness observations, explaining precisely the evidence that the witness may be capable of testifying about in court.
5.   CROWN BRIEF:
- a written record of existing evidence which supports a charge against an accused person.
- it is prepared by the police and submitted to the Crown Attorney.
- it will be disclosed to the defence/accused person to comply with section 7 Charter.
- it is composed of two primary parts:
  - (i)   Summary:
    a narration of the incident that explains the facts and circumstances (evidence) and proves the facts in issue of the offence. Therefore, the summary must establish a *prima facie case*.
  - (ii)   Witness Statements

2

General Principles

Police reports vary in nature and content. The nature ranges from murders to provincial offences; the content is determined by the events learned through investigations. The content of each police report will have its own unique set of circumstances. Therefore, the specific facts reported will not be the same in all reports.

Despite the wide ranging differences of police reports, general principles can be applied, to any report or notebook recording, which will elevate its quality. Principles are general rules that will assist the writer of a police report to effectively construct and include all relevant details to properly inform the reader of an occurence. These report writing principles will be listed and explained in this chapter. They will be further explained in subsequent chapters as they apply to a specific type of report.

PRINCIPLES OF REPORT WRITING

1. The goal of report writing is to re-create an occurence or observation in its entirety, to eliminate confusion and loss of relevant information. The reader must be informed of all details, whether major or minor. The writing should cause the reader to form a mental image or picture of the entire event.

2. Assume the reader has absolutely no knowledge of the occurrence, involved people, or the location of the incident. This will force the writer to describe events, people and places in a specific rather than a general manner.

3. Assume that no other source of communication will exist between the writer and the reader. The writer should never assume that he/she will have another opportunity to inform the reader about additional facts. Following this principle will prevent the omission of relevant information, precise descriptions or explanations.

4. Assume that no opportunity exists to verbally communicate to the reader in order to clarify information. This will prevent vagueness and complacency in relating details.

5. When describing an event or observation, avoid using general terms that represent the shore form name of the offence, e.g., assault, theft, rob, damaged. The terms are the conclusions that the writer intends the reader to make. For example, avoid writing, "Bill assaulted Helen." This does not re-create the occurrence. It only states the outcome. Instead, describe the specific act committed, such as, "Bill clenched his right fist and walked toward Helen. Bill raised his fist and struck Helen's chin." The reader can create a specific mental image and conclude that an assault occurred.

6. Avoid paraphrasing. Paraphrasing means the condensing an observation to a minimal explanation. Paraphrasing is a brief summary which lacks specific details and causes the reader to ask questions

5

about the incident. An example of paraphrasing is, "Ralph saw Bill hit Helen." Several questions can be asked by the reader, including:
-where was Ralph when he made the observation?
-where was Bill?
-how exactly did Bill hit Helen?
-who are Ralph, Bill and Helen?
-what did Bill say before or after the offence?
The reader should have no questions after reading a report.

7.   All relevant conversation should be recorded verbatim. Verbatim means word-for-word direct quotes. Conversation includes:
a) verbal information stated or asked by an officer to a suspect or accused, including:
-reason for arrest
-right to counsel
-wording of the caution
-breathalizer demands
-request for consent
When a writer intends to inform the reader that the above remarks wer made, he/she is asking the reader to make a conclusion. This can only be achieved by informing the reader of the verbatim conversation. For example, simply writing, "I asked for consent to search," raises the question, "What exactly was asked? Were any threats made?" By writing the verbatim conversation, the reader will be able to conclude whether or not valid consent was asked for.
b) statements and responses made by suspects or accused persons, including:
-confessions and admissions
-answers to questions
Fox example, after informing an arrested person of the right to counsel, or, cautioning th person, the question, "Do you understand?" is asked. If the accused says, "Yes," that response should be written. Do not write, "The accused understood." Avoiding the latter phrase will prevent the reader from asking, "How can it be proven that the accused understood?" or, "What exactly did the accused say?"
Confessions are crucial forms of evidence which help prove guilt beyond reasonable doubt. Avoid writing, "He confessed." This is a conclusion that the reader has to make. Writing the verbatim quote is crucial because it will be necessary to state this during testimony at the trial. A judge will ultimately decide whether the verbatim statement represents incriminating evidence and is actually a confession.

8.   If multiple witnesses report observations during an investigation, write each individual observation separately. Avoid writing group observations such as, "They saw", or "They heard." The reader must conclude that each person in the group heard or saw the same thing and then evaluate the credibility of each witness individually.
Each witness will have to testify separately in court. Therefore, all reports must reflect the individual observations.

9.   The report of a person's observation must be followed by the presence or absence of factors that may have affected the observation. Examples include:
-distance
-objects interfering with sight
-sounds interfering with hearing
-physical condition, such as impairment
The reader's evaluation of the witness's credibility will be facilitated by including not only the presence of such factors, but also the absence of them.

10. Include each witness's capability of facially recognizing a suspect or accused person. Facial recognition represents one method of identifying a person. The reader must know whether each individual witness can or cannot identify a suspect or accused person.

11. Describe all geographic locations in detail. For example, if an incident occurred at the intersection of King and Lincoln Streets, assume that the reader has absolutely no knowledge of this area. This will force the writer to describe the location in detail to give the reader a vivid mental image of the entire surroundings.

12. Describe places that are mentioned in a report. When an incident occurs in a place, such as a house or business premises, describe it sufficiently to the reader and include:
>-type (buisness or residence)
>-number of floors and rooms
>-entrances
>-dimensions of the room where the incident occurred
>-objects in the room

A rough diagram may be used to accompany the written description.

13. Physical evidence must be described in a manner that would allow any person, including someone who is unfamiliar with the item, to positively identify it. Positive identification means recognizing an item beyond reasonable doublt. This can be accomplished by including in the report:
>a) general description
>>-type of item
>>-make, model
>>-colour
>>-size

General descriptions will not permit positive identification.
>b) specific description
>>-any unique feature that is exclusive to the item
>>-serial number
>>-damage
>>-wear marks

Specific descriptions permit positive identification.

14. Describe suspects sufficiently to allow any person to positively identify or recognize him or her. Include:
>a) general description
>>-gender
>>-height and weight
>>-build type
>>-hair and eye colour
>>-presence or absence of facial hair
>>-clothing; type and colour
>b) specific description
>>-unique features such as:
>>>-scars
>>>-tattoos
>>>-writing on clothing

15. The reader should have no questions to ask the writer after a report is read. This signifies that all facts and details have been explained. If this is achieved, the writer has fulfilled the intended goal.

3

General Occurrence Report (G.O.R.)

Principles and Procedures: The General Occurrence Report (G.O.R.) represents the standard police report. A G.O.R. is written when a complainant/victim reports an incident to the police. Subject to respective police force policies, minor incidents may no longer be documented on G.O.R.'s.

The subject of G.O.R.'s may include criminal offences, provincial offences, disputes not constituting an offence, missing persons and sudden deaths.

In usual circumstances, a uniform patrol officer is the *first officer* at a crime scene and has initial contact with the complainant/victim. The responsibility of writing the initial G.O.R. usually rests with the *first officer*.

After conducting a preliminary or initial investigation, the first officer explains the facts and circumstances of the occurrence up to that stage. In many police departments, the first officer does not continue an investigation unless the following circumstances exist:

- the officer has attained the necessary investigative skills and expertise;
- the amount of investigation time will not adversely affect patrol coverage of a district;
- the investigation will not require the officer to travel extensively out of his/her patrol area;
- the offence is not classified as major.

In many situations, patrol demands prohibit the first officer from continuing an investigation. Consequently, the investigative responsibilities are usually transferred to a detective (a member of the Criminal Investigation Branch). This procedure adds to the significance of proper report writing because the initial G.O.R. is submitted by the first officer for assignment to an investigator.

The G.O.R. is the *primary means of communication* between the first officer and the investigator. Incomplete or inaccurate reports may cause the investigator to unnecessarily repeat part of the investigation or to be uninformed of relevant information.

Additionally, the investigator's job essentially is to *formulate reasonable grounds* to arrest and charge the offender. The information written in the initial G.O.R. is a crucial factor in the process of reasonable grounds formulation, not only in relation to arrests and charges but also regarding searches for evidence, with and without a warrant.

Often, no verbal communication occurs between the first officer and the investigator. Therefore, the objective of a G.O.R. is to provide a *primary method of communication*. Consequently, the report must convey an *extensive re-creation of the occurrence* in order to eliminate confusion and loss of relevant information.

Accordingly, the *first two principles* of report writing are *assumptions* that should be maintained by the writer during the composition of a report.

The writer should *assume*:

    (i)   the reader of the report has absolutely *no knowledge* of the occurrence and has *no other source of communication* to rely on for knowledge, other than the G.O.R., and

    (ii)   the writer will never have the opportunity to add information or clarify written details by means of verbal communication with the reader.

These assumptions may increase the extensiveness and preciseness of the report by creating the writer's awareness of vagueness, ambiguities and insufficient facts or descriptions.

The G.O.R. is composed of two parts:

    (i)   cover page

    (ii)   narrative

Cover Page: this page requires filling in the blanks to inform the reader about the following:

- *nature* of the report (type of offence, i.e., robbery)
- *time*, *date* and *location* of incident
- *complainant/victim's* personal information (including condition, e.g., sobriety)
- personal information of *person reporting incident*
- *suspect's* personal information and description
- brief description and value of stolen or damaged *property*
- description of *vehicle*, if any, used in the incident
- name of *officer* who wrote the report
- names of all officers attending at the scene
- *time* the report was taken
- report number

The cover page informs the reader about essential introductory facts. If the spaces provided are insufficient, such as the *property* section, print "see narrative" and describe the property in that portion of the G.O.R.

The investigator uses the cover page for two reasons:

    (i)   to gain familiarity about the names of the involved persons and the location of the incident.

    (ii)   to form preliminary *opinions* about:

        • *credibility* of the complainant (e.g., intoxicated)

        • *validity* of the reported offence (i.e., possibility of fabrication)

This opinion is formed by:

- analyzing the time and location of offence combined with quantity of property stolen or damaged, and
- comparing time of incident and time of report; any unreasonable delay may require justification.

Narrative: This portion is the formal, written explanation of the facts and circumstances that compose the incident. The *narrative* essentially is the written police report; it is the portion of the report that requires writing skills based on principles and procedures.

The narrative is written on *supplementary* reports. These essentially are lined paper with headings at the top that must be completed to correspond with the information on the cover page (e.g., report number, nature of complaint, complainant's name and address).

Narratives vary with different types of occurrences. The differences depend on whether:

- the crime is in relation to a *person* or to *property*.
- a suspect does *not* exist.
- a suspect exists but his/her identity is *unknown*.
- a suspect exists and his/her identity is *known*.

Regardless of the variances that may exist about the occurrences that are reported to police, a *general format* should be used for *all* narratives.

General Format - The narrative consists of four phases, written in chronological order:

    (i)   introduction
    (ii)   events *before* the crime
    (iii)   events *during* the crime
    (iv)   events *after* the crime

Depending on police force policy, the following procedures are sometimes preferred:

- narrative should be written in the *third person*
- times should be recorded according to the 24 hour system
- (e.g., 1300 hrs. is 1:00 p.m)
- dates should be written metrically (i.e., year-month-day.)

(i)   **Introduction (first phase):** The introduction serves the following purposes:

(a)   it permits the investigator an opportunity to form an *initial opinion* regarding the *validity* of the offence reported. Validating the offence is the first step in the investigative sequence. For example, an investigator should determine whether the offence actually occurred or whether it was fabricated. Fabricated offences are reported for several reasons (i.e., reporting a false theft to defraud an insurance company.)

(b)   *specific questions* should be answered to facilitate the formation of an initial validity opinion and to provide a structured introduction of all relevant information that will prevent confusion for the investigator when reading the narrative. The specific questions are:

- Where was the report taken?
- *the investigator needs to know if the offence was reported at the crime scene or if it was reported elsewhere (e.g., at the police station). An indicator of an invalid complaint may be reporting an offence at a location other than the crime scene. If the complaint is valid and the offence was reported elsewhere, the investigator will know that the crime scene may have been left unprotected. The investigator will have to prove that the crime scene and any physical evidence found there was not altered or destroyed.*

Example #1:

> At 22:45 hrs., 93-01-04, Cst. Friendly attended at 1000 King Street, Welland, in response to a break, enter and theft.
>
> or
>
> At 22:45 hrs., 93-01-04, Gord Smythe attended at the Welland police station to report a break, enter and theft that occurred at his house.

- Who met the police to report the offence?
- *If the complainant was not the person reporting the offence, the investigator will know that another potential witness exists and the victim/ complainant did not provide the initial facts. The reason for this will later have to be explored. The facts reported by someone other than the victim/ complainant may be incomplete.*

Example #2:

> Upon arrival, the officer was met by Gord Smythe, the complainant in this matter.
>
> Or
>
> Upon arrival, the officer was met by Leon Robins, a witness in this matter. Gord Smythe, the complainant, had been transported to the hospital by ambulance.

After answering these two questions, the *complainant* and all involved persons (i.e., suspect, if any) should be introduced. In order to structure the introductions for the reader, the following sentence should precede it:

Example #3:

> Gord reported the following to police:

The introduction should briefly summarize the individual's personal information, to allow the investigator to form a perception of the person:

Example #4:

> Gord is <u>40</u> years old. He is the <u>owner</u> of a dwelling <u>house</u> situated at <u>1000 King St.</u>, <u>Welland</u>. He is <u>legally</u> <u>married</u> to June. They have two sons, Wally, age 18 years, and Robert, age 15 years. Gord is employed at Niagara College where he holds the position of librarian. June is employed at Niagara College where she holds the position of professor.

This example informs the investigator of the following facts:
- *the identity of the <u>owner</u>*: necessary for the court trial, after the charge is laid.
- *Gord and June are <u>legally married</u>*: this affects their competency to testify against each other should the investigation reveal that one of them, or both, intentionally fabricated the report resulting in a charge of *public mischief.*
- *they have two sons*: if the report is valid, the investigator's next phase is to suspect relatives. In this example, the investigator must be cognizant that the sons *may* have some involvement in the planning of the break and enter, either intentionally or unintentionally.
- *the occupational status of Gord and June*: allows the investigator to form an *opinion* about the presence or absence of a motive for fabricating this occurrence because *validating* the occurrence is the *first phase* of the investigation.

The final part of the introduction may be information about a *known* suspect. If the suspect's identity is known, the investigator should be advised of this fact in the introduction. Additionally, the issue of *facial recognition* should be addressed at this stage. A prominent fact in issue at the trial will be the accused's *identity*. Therefore, the investigator must be informed of *who* may be capable of facially recognizing the accused person as being the individual who actually committed the offence.

Example #5:

> The suspect in this matter is Eddie Hopkins, age 18 years. He lives at 1002 King Street, Welland, next door to the Smythe's. Wally has known Eddie for 10 years.

In this example, the investigator will know that Wally will be easily capable of facially recognizing the suspect. After the introduction is complete, the writer begins the second phase of the narrative.

(ii)   **Events Before the Offence (second phase):** This phase must extensively describe *relevant* facts or circumstances that occurred *before* the commission of the offence. *Relevant facts or circumstances* include:
- *anything related to a fact in issue of the offence reported.*
- *any communication between the suspect and the victim or any witnesses, before the suspect committed the offence. The primary issues that require attention are:*
  - (i)   *facial recognition* of the suspect,
    and
  - (ii) *verbal statements* made by the suspects. Verbal statements may help prove the suspect's *mens rea* (intent to commit the offence). Any statements should be recorded verbatim, meaning *word for word (quotation)*, not by paraphrasing.
- *factors affecting observations of all witnesses, including complainant/ victim. For example, alcohol or drug use and whether the witness had the* intent to learn *before the offence occurred. The* presence or absence *of these factors will significantly contribute to the investigator's evaluation of witness credibility. The evaluations are a critical determinant in the* formulation of reasonable grounds.

The narrative of this phase commonly begins on the offence date but it may be extended to any previous date that will include a *relevant fact or circumstance*.

Example #6:

> During December 1993, Wally accumulated large debts. On December 15th, Wally met Eddie at Eddie's house. Wally asked Eddie to lend him $500.00 and Eddie agreed. Wally informed Eddie that he would reimburse him on December 31. However, Wally failed to repay Eddie on that day.
>
> On 94-01-03, Wally left his house at 08:00 hrs. Eddie was in his driveway next door. Eddie yelled to Wally, "You better pay me back today, jerk." Wally entered his car and drove to Niagara College where he attended classes until 16:30 hrs. He consumed no alcohol or drugs during the day.
>
> Wally drove home and arrived at 16:45 hrs. He entered the kitchen and sat down at the table to read a newspaper.
>
> At that time, Eddie entered the kitchen via the back door. He stood in the doorway, about 10 feet from Wally. Eddie held a wooden baseball bat at his side, in his right hand and said, "Give me my money." Wally replied, "Get lost. I haven't got it."

In this example, the investigator is informed:
- of the suspect's *possession of a weapon*
- of *verbatim verbal statements* that may help prove an **intention** to assault Wally (mens rea)
- of the suspect's *motive* for intending to assault Wally
- that Wally was capable of *facially recognizing* the suspect
- that Wally was sober
- that Wally has the *intent to learn* the events that are about to occur. Wally's attention to the circumstances qualifies him as an *intentional learner*. Consequently, he should acquire numerous observations.
- that Wally has an unobstructed view.
- that no factors apparently affected Wally's observations.

The investigator would then have sufficient information to form opinions of:
- (a) Wally's credibility, and
- (b) reasonable grounds formulation, up to this point of the explanation.

At the completion of this phase, the writer begins the third phase to describe the *events during the offence*.

(iii)   Events During the Offence (third phase):   This phase must accurately and specifically describe the *actus reus* (physical act) of the offence.

The format and extensiveness of this phase of the narrative depends on whether the offence *was witnessed* or *was not witnessed*.

A narrative that explains an offence that *was witnessed*, will be a re-creation of the physical acts that constituted the offence. An offence that is *not witnessed*, for example, a break and enter, will not have an extensive narrative describing the actual physical act. Instead, a comprehensive narrative will be required to describe the *crime scene*, before and after the offence occurred. Essentially, the investigator combines the narrative in *phase 2* (*before the offence*) with *phase 4* (*after the offence*) to form opinions, inferences or conclusions about the physical act that constituted the offence.

Similar principles are used to write both types of narratives for this phase.

The following nine *principles* may be used to write this narrative phase:

1. *Determine the facts in issue of the offence being reported. In other words, the writer must determine the actus reus that composes the offence.*
2. *The narrative must be relevant to the* facts in issue *of the offence.*
3. *Avoid using general terms that are used in the short form name of the offence (e.g., break and enter). Instead, describe the circumstances precisely to allow the investigator to make an inference or conclusion that the offence occurred. Examples of terms to avoid are:*

   - assault   - steal   -threatened
   - theft   - rob   -damaged
   - intoxicated   - break and enter.

   These terms may be used to introduce or summarize the narrative.
4. *Avoid paraphrasing because it prevents the reader from accurately forming reasonable grounds. The writer's objective is to transfer reasonable grounds in writing. If the writer paraphrases by using general terms such as assault, the reader is unable to form reasonable grounds that each fact in issue of the offence existed. Paraphrasing causes vagueness and ambiguity by omitting the specific acts that compose the facts in issue. Eliminating paraphrasing is an effective method to increase relevant details.*

5.   *Write verbatim quotations regarding any verbal statements made by a suspect. A suspect's verbal statement may constitute a confession, representing crucial evidence that may prove guilt beyond a reasonable doubt. In some cases a suspect's verbatim statement may be the only direct means of proving mens rea or other facts in issue. Paraphrasing may hinder reasonable grounds formulation by the investigator. The investigator is required to determine whether verbal statements are inculpatory and will contribute to reasonable grounds formulation. A paraphrased verbal statement prevents the investigator from making these conclusions.*

6.   *If multiple witnesses exist who saw the actus reus, each individual witness's observation must be recorded separately. This allows the investigator to evaluate the credibility of each witness. One explanation that combines all witness observations prevents the investigator from making initial credibility evaluations. Witnesses commonly report inaccurate observations, either intentionally or unintentionally, thereby creating the need for separate narratives. If the observations differ, the investigator is responsible to evaluate the credibility of each witness and attempt to form reasonable grounds on that basis.*

7.   *Include any factors that may affect the observations of the witness. The investigator's evaluation of witness credibility is contingent upon ten factors including, the witness's relative position when the observation was made, intent to learn before the observation and sobriety. If the observation is unaffected, the writer should state that adverse factors were absent.*

8.   *State whether each witness can facially recognize the suspect.*

9.   *Physical evidence must be described in a manner that would allow any person, including someone who is unfamiliar with the item, to positively identify it. Positive identification refers to recognizing an item beyond reasonable doubt. This can be accomplished by including the following elements in descriptions:*

General Description	***Specific Description***
- specific type of item	- any unique feature that
-make, model	is exclusive to the item
-size	e.g., damage, wear marks.
-colour	or serial number

The degree of uniqueness increases the possibility of positive identification. Therefore, the description should be focused upon features that only that particular item has.

The following examples demonstrate how the actus reus of a break and enter may be explained when *no witnesses* exist:

Example #7 (before the offence):

> Gord left his house at 08:00 hrs. He locked the doors and secured the house. He drove to Niagara College and arrived there at 08:15 hrs. Gord worked until 16:30 hrs. He returned home and arrived home at 16:45 hrs.

Example #8 (after the offence):

At that time Gord discovered that the rear door was open. The door is wooden, 7 feet high, 3 feet wide, and leads into the kitchen. Shoeprints were visible on the surface near the doorknob but the shoeprint tread was NOT discernible. The wooden frame was cracked and splintered near the door latch. The cost of repairing the damage is about $250.00.

The Smythe residence has only one floor and a basement. The house consists of a kitchen, living room, a washroom and three bedrooms on the main floor. A recreation room and a laundry room are situated in the basement.

A television set and a V.C.R. were missing from the living room. The drawers in Gord and June's bedroom were found open. A watch and $300.00 in cash were missing from inside the top drawer.

Nothing else in the house apparently was touched. The missing items, which were reported stolen, are described as follows:
- 20" SONY colour television set ;
  - grey and black frame
  - serial #123456
  - a 2" dent on the speaker screen, next to the screen.
  - the remote control was not stolen
    - **value = $500.00**
- J.V.C. videocassette recorder (V.H.S.)
  - black frame
  - serial #654321
  - one screw missing from the top, where the frame connects with the front screen plate.
    - **value = $400.00**
- man's "VETTA" wristwatch
  - gold frame
  - white surface
  - black roman numerals
  - date indicator instead of the digit "six"
  - brown leather band with gold buckle
  - on back of watch:
    - "SWISS MADE", printed
    - "WATER RESISTANT", printed
    - triangle symbol in middle
      - **value = $250.00**
- $300.00 cash
  - Canadian currency
  - denominations =
    - 1- $100.00 bills
    - 2- $50.00 bills
    - 5- $20.00 bills

TOTAL VALUE = $1,450.00

The events during the offence (third phase) was accomplished by describing the events before and after the offence. The principles used in Examples #7 & 8 informed the investigator of the following:

- the point of entry. Rather than paraphrasing, "The suspect *broke* into the house by *forcibly opening* the back door", the description creates the inference that the fact in issue "break", occurred. The paraphrase is inadequate for an investigator to form reasonable grounds about this fact in issue.
- that property is missing. This creates two inferences. First, "**entry**" was gained. Secondly, "**theft**" occurred.
- that the missing items are identifiable. The descriptions included unique features of the items.
- the specific items that were handled or touched by the suspect. This assists the Identification officer when examining the scene for fingerprints. If the writer is satisfied that no other items had been touched, a summary statement should be included stating, "No other items have been touched."
- the time the house was locked and the time of discovery. This creates the boundaries for the offence time.
- a description of the house. This gives the investigator a way to form an initial opinion about the *validity* of the complaint and about similarities with methods used by certain offenders who have committed previous break and enters.

The general terms *break*, *enter* and *theft* or *stole* may be used to summarize or introduce the narrative but avoidance of the terms compels the writer to describe precisely the crime scene and prevents the omission of valuable facts.

Offences that are *witnessed* require narratives that utilize the same nine principles. To reiterate the most important principle to ensure comprehensiveness:

- avoid using the **name** of an offence to explain a witness's observations. The words **assaulted**, **threatened**, **damaged** or **stole** are inadequate in the narrative for the purpose of informing the reader about the facts and circumstances during the offence. The offence name may be used to introduce or summarize witness observation but should not be used as the sole description of the events during the crime. Paraphrasing interferes with reasonable grounds formulation.

Example #9:

Avoid:	The suspect **threatened** her.
Use :	The suspect said, "I'm going to kill you."
Avoid:	The suspect **assaulted** her.
Use :	The suspect punched her in the jaw with his right fist.
Avoid:	The suspect **stole** the cassette tape.
Use :	The suspect removed the cassette tape from the second shelf of aisle B and put the tape in his right jacket pocket.
Avoid:	The suspect was **intoxicated**.
Use :	The suspect's breath smelled of an alcoholic beverage, his eyes were bloodshot, his speech was slurred and he banged into the walls twice while he walked.

Instead of using the offence name, the writer must **precisely describe the act** that constituted the offence without using single words that refer to a type of offence. Reasonable grounds formulation is dependent upon the specificly of the explanation.

Adhering to these principles will prevent the investigator from unnecessarily interviewing witnesses about issues that were initially reported and will significantly facilitate the investigator's formulation of reasonable grounds.

The following example is a continuation of example #6, that illustrates the use of these principles to explain an offence witnessed by the complainant:

Example #10:

> Eddie walked toward Wally and stood about two feet from him. Wally remained seated. Eddie raised the bat, held it in both hands and positioned it inches from Wally's face while he said, "I said, pay me my money or I'll bust you up." Wally rose from his chair, stood in front of Eddie and replied, "Get out of my house or I'll call the cops."
> Eddie swung the bat, striking the right side of Wally's torso.

After the events *during* the offence are explained, the writer begins the final phase of the narrative - events *after* the offence.

(iv)　**Events After the Offence (fourth phase):** This phase must comprehensively describe *relevant* facts and circumstances that occurred between the *time that the actual offence ended* and the *time that the first officer's preliminary investigation concluded.*

The following principles may be used to explain the relevant facts and circumstances:

- anything that may prove a fact in issue related to the reported offence. This includes:
  - (a) describing the crime scene sufficiently to allow the reader to visualize its appearance. Afterward, the writer must explain what evidence may have been *transferred by the suspect to the crime scene* (e.g., fingerprints, shoeprints, weapons) or *by the suspect from the crime scene* (e.g., stolen property).
  - (b) the disposal of any evidence that proves at least one *fact in issue*. For example, the suspect may have been seen concealing weapons or offering to sell stolen property. Complete observations and verbatim statements must be included in this phase to describe these events.
- any communication between the suspect and the complainant/victim or any witness, *after* the commission of the offence. All verbal statements made by the suspect must be written *verbatim*. These statements represent potential confessions that will allow the investigator to form reasonable grounds. Paraphrasing a suspect's verbal statement may not constitute a confession and may lower its value from reasonable grounds to mere suspicion. Additionally, the witness's capability of facially recognizing the suspect must be included in the narrative.
- factors affecting observations of all witnesses, including the complainant/victim. The writer should report the *presence or absence* of certain factors, including:
  - alcohol or drugs
  - injuries
  - position of the witness
  - intent to learn

- accurate means and direction of departure and possible *destinations* of the suspect (if the suspect left the crime scene prior to police arrival). The grounds for this belief must be specified (i.e., witness's direct observation or mere speculation or conjecture). If departure or destination information is *unknown*, this fact must be clearly stated.

- the presence or absence of weapons in the suspect's possession. If a weapon was seen by a witness, the weapon must be described as accurately and precisely as possible. Additionally, it is imperative to include witness observations that accurately explain whether the suspect retained possession of the weapon upon departure. *If weapons were not seen, the writer should not conclude, "The suspect was unarmed." Instead, the writer should state, "No one saw the accused possessing a weapon."*

The following is an example of a narrative using these principles. The example is a continuation of Example #10:

Example #11:

> Wally saw Eddie immediately run out the back door. Eddie kept possession of the bat as he departed. His direction of travel was not seen by Wally. Wally did not hear a car leaving the area. Wally subsequently phoned the police and an ambulance.
>
> Cst. Friendly arrived at the Smythe residence at 16:50 hrs. Ambulance attendants were present and were treating Wally. Wally was conscious and briefly reported the incident.
>
> Wally was transported to the hospital. Dr. Smith's examination revealed that Wally suffered two broken ribs. Wally was interviewed at 17:15 hrs. at the hospital and gave a signed, written statement to Cst. Friendly.
>
> At 17:30 hrs., Cst. Friendly attended at the Haskell residence. No one was home.
>
> At 17:45 hrs., Cst. Friendly attended at 1100 King Street in response to a call from Mitchell Rutherford. He was interviewed and gave a signed, written statement reporting the following:
>
> Mitchell has known Eddie for 10 years. They are neighbours and classmates. At 17:30 hrs. on this date, Eddie attended at the Rutherford residence. Eddie had possession of a wooden baseball bat. Eddie told Mitchell, "Hide this bat in your basement. I just pounded Wally and I think I broke his ribs. The cops are probably looking for me."
>
> Eddie gave the bat to Mitchell. Mitchell asked, "Where are you going?" Eddie replied, "I'm driving to Toronto. If the cops talk to you, tell them I was in Toronto all day."
>
> Cst. Friendly asked Mitchell if he would consent to the seizure of the bat even though consent was not obligatory or irrevocable. Mitchell voluntarily gave the bat to Cst. Friendly.

Phase 4 may extend to include any other witness observations or investigative procedure that occurred.

Conclusion: If the suspect is not arrested by the first officer during the preliminary investigation or if a suspect is unknown, the writer may conclude the narrative by writing a conclusion that is directed toward an investigative sequence that may benefit the investigator.

When a suspect is unknown, the following stages are a useful sequence that may be used to investigate any offence:

      (i)   validating the offence

      (ii)   suspecting relatives of victim/complainant

      (iii) suspecting acquaintances or persons who have gained familiarity with the complainant.

      (iv) suspecting a person unfamiliar with the complainant.

Accordingly, the writer may state an opinion about the validity of the complaint supported by the reasons for the opinion. If the complaint is considered valid, the writer should include names and addresses of persons in the second and third categories of the investigative sequence, with a notation alerting the investigator about whether or not they have been interviewed. The phrase "investigation continues" concludes the first officer's G.O.R.

After the G.O.R. is completed, the report is submitted to a supervisor for examination. If the investigation will be continued by a C.I.B. Officer, the G.O.R. is assigned to an investigator.

Examples:

Break and Enter - G.O.R. (suspect unknown - property offence)

> At 22:45 hrs., 94-01-04, Cst. Friendly attended at 1000 King Street, Welland, in response to a break, enter and theft.
>
> Upon arrival, the officer was met by Gord Smythe, the complainant in this matter.
>
> Gord is 40 years old. He is the owner of a dwelling house situated at 1000 King St., Welland. He is legally married to June. They have two sons, Wally, age 18 years, and Robert, age 15 years. Gord is employed at Niagara College where he holds the position of librarian. June is employed at Niagara College where she holds the position of professor.
>
> Gord reported the following to police:
>
> Gord left his house at 08:00 hrs. He locked the doors and secured the house. He drove to Niagara College and arrived there at 08:15 hrs. Gord worked until 16:30 hrs. He returned home and arrived home at 16:45 hrs.
>
> At that time Gord discovered that the rear door was open. The door is wooden, 7 feet high, 3 feet wide and leads to the kitchen. Shoeprints were visible on the surface near the doorknob but the shoeprint tread was NOT discernible. The wooden frame was damaged near the door latch. The cost of repairing the damage is about $250.00.
>
> The Smythe residence has only one floor and a basement. The house consists of a kitchen, living room, a washroom and three bedrooms on the main floor. A recreation room and a laundry room are situated in the basement.
>
> A television set and a V.C.R. were missing from the living room. The drawers in Gord and June's bedroom were found open. A watch and $300.00 in cash were missing from inside the top drawer.
>
> Nothing else in the house apparently was touched. The missing items, which were reported stolen, are described as follows:
>
>   •   20" SONY colour television set;
>   - grey and black frame
>   - serial #123456

B & E (con't)

- a 2" dent on the speaker screen, next to the screen.
- the remote control was not stolen
  - **value = $500.00**
- J.V.C. videocassette recorder (V.H.S.)
  - black frame
  - serial #654321
  - one screw missing from the top, where the frame connects with the front screen plate.
    - **value = $400.00**
- man's "VETTA" wristwatch
  - gold frame
  - white surface
  - black roman numerals
  - date indicator instead of the digit "six"
  - brown leather band with gold buckle
  - on back of watch:
    - "SWISS MADE", printed
    - "WATER RESISTANT", printed
    - triangle symbol in middle
    - **value = $250.00**
- $300.00 cash
  - Canadian currency
  - denominations =
    - 1 - $100.00 bills
    - 2 - $50.00 bills
    - 5 - $20.00 bills
    - **TOTAL VALUE = $1,450.00**

INVESTIGATION CONTINUES

Assault - G.O.R. (crime vs. person - suspect known)

The suspect in this matter is Eddie Hopkins, age 18 years. He lives at 1002 King Street, Welland, next door to the Smythes. Wally has known Eddie for 10 years.

During December 1993, Wally accumulated large debts. On December 15th, Wally met Eddie at Eddie's house. Wally asked Eddie to lend him $500.00 and Eddie agreed. Wally informed Eddie that he would reimburse him on December 31. However, Wally failed to repay Eddie on that day.

On 94-01-03, Wally left his residence at 1004 King Street, at 08:00 hrs. Eddie was in his driveway next door. Eddie yelled to Wally, "You better pay me back today, jerk." Wally entered his car and drove to Niagara College where he attended classes until 16:30 hrs. He consumed no alcohol or drugs during the day.

Wally drove home and arrived at 16:45 hrs. He entered the kitchen and sat down at the table to read a newspaper.

At that time, Eddie entered the kitchen via the back door. He stood in the doorway, about ten feet from Wally. Eddie held a wooden baseball bat at his side, in his right hand and said "Give me my money." Wally replied, "Get lost. I haven't got it."

Eddie walked toward Wally and stood about two feet from him. Wally remained seated. Eddie raised the bat, held it in both hands and positioned it inches

Assault (con't)

from Wally's face while he said, "I said, pay me my money or I'll bust you up." Wally rose from his chair, stood in front of Eddie and replied, "Get out of my house or I'll call the cops."

Eddie swung the bat, striking the right side of Wally's torso.

Wally saw Eddie immediately run out the back door. Eddie kept possession of the bat as he departed. His direction of travel was not seen by Wally. Wally did not hear a car leaving the area. Wally subsequently phoned the police and an ambulance.

Cst. Friendly arrived at the Smythe residence at 16:50 hrs. Ambulance attendants were present and were treating Wally. Wally was conscious and briefly reported the incident.

Wally was transported to the hospital. Dr. Smith's examination revealed that Wally suffered two broken ribs. Wally was interviewed at 17:15 hrs. at the hospital and gave a signed, written statement to Cst. Friendly.

At 17:30 hrs., Cst. Friendly attended at the Hopkins residence. No one was home.

At 17:45 hrs., Cst. Friendly attended at 1100 King Street in response to a call from Mitchell Rutherford. He was interviewed and gave a signed, written statement reporting the following:

Mitchell has known Eddie for 10 years, they are neighbours and classmates. At 17:30 hrs. on this date, Eddie attended at the Rutherford residence. Eddie had possession of a wooden baseball bat. Eddie told Mitchell, "Hide this bat in your basement. I just pounded Wally and I think I broke his ribs. The cops are probably looking for me."

Eddie gave the bat to Mitchell. Mitchell asked, "Where are you going?" Eddie replied, "I'm driving to Toronto. If the cops talk to you, tell them I was in Toronto all day."

Cst. Friendly asked Mitchell if he would consent to the seizure of the bat even though consent was not obligatory or irrevocable. Mitchell voluntarily gave the bat to Cst. Friendly.

INVESTIGATION CONTINUES

Missing Person - G.O.R.

At 18:00 hrs., 94-01-06, Cst. Friendly attended at 1000 King Street, Welland regarding a missing person. Upon arrival, the officer was met by June Smythe, who reported the following to police:

June is 40 years old. She lives at 1000 King Street, Welland with her legally married husband, Gord, and two sons, Wally (age 18 years) and Timothy (age 15 years). June is employed at Niagara College where she holds the position of professor.

Timothy Smythe, D.O.B.. 78-11-15, the missing person, was described as follows:

- male/white, 5'5" tall, 150 lbs., light brown short hair, parted on the left side, brown eyes.

At 07:45 hrs., on this date, the Smythe family ate breakfast together in their kitchen. June and Gord had a brief conversation about how June dreaded having

Missing Person (con't)

classes start again. Wally and Timothy did not participate in the conversation. After they finished eating, Wally and Timothy left the house together. Both are students at Churchill High School, situated at 5000 Main Street, Welland. Timothy is a grade 10 student there. They routinely walk to school together, every morning. Timothy wore the following clothes today:

- a grey long sleeve sweatshirt with "Churchill football" printed in red letters on the front
- grey sweat pants with a red bulldog printed on the front of the left thigh
- grey bomber jacket with "Churchill Football" printed in red letters on the back, the letters "RB" on the right sleeve in red and the numbers "33" printed on the left sleeve
- black NIKE running shoes
- white sweat socks
- blue gym bag

Timothy had no argument with any family member during breakfast. He appeared to be in his normal good mood. He displayed no unusual behaviour. He did not say that he had plans after school.

Classes at Churchill begin at 08:55 hrs. and end at 15:20 hrs..

June arrived home from work at 15:50 hrs. No one was home.

Wally arrived home at 16:10 hrs., alone. Wally saw Timothy at his locker at 15:30 hrs. but Wally did not speak to him.

June phoned the school at 16:45 hrs. and spoke to the Vice-Principal, Mrs. Smith. June was informed that the school was vacant but Timothy had attended every class during the day.

At 17:50 hrs., June phone police after Timothy had not returned home.

Timothy had no known after school activities. He is a member of the football team but that activity ended two months previously, in November.

No family arguments have occurred recently. Timothy has displayed no unusual behaviour such as depression. The following is a list of names and addresses of Timothy's known friends: (list information).

INVESTIGATION CONTINUES

4

Supplementary Report

After the initial G.O.R. is submitted, any subsequent investigation is recorded on the same supplementary reports used for all four phases of the initial G.O.R. narrative. These reports, also known as "follow-up reports", must include, the initial report number, the complainant's name and address and the nature of the complaint. This information is printed in the appropriate boxes at the top of each page of the supplementary report.

The narrative portion of each supplementary report should begin with the following introductory phrase:

Example #12:

> "Further to the report of (original officer's name):"

Writing supplementary narratives involves the use of the *same principles* as those associated with the G.O.R. During the investigation witnesses who are interviewed after the offence may give evidence relating to *before*, *during* or *after* the crime. Consequently, the format used in each supplementary will be the one governed by which phase of the offence that the observation is relevant to.

If an investigation is *unsolved*, the final supplementary page will conclude with the phrase, **"Investigation continues."**

If an investigation results in a *solved offence*, three possible conclusions exist, noted by the following phrases:

Example #13:

- "CLEARED BY CHARGE" (refers to an information being sworn - the accused has been formally charged.)

- "CLEARED OTHERWISE" (the offence did occur but no charges will be laid; the offence was solved in **another** manner.)

- "CLEARED - UNFOUNDED" (the offence did not occur.)

Regardless of when the arrest is made, the *narrative principles and format* are the same. The only difference is that an arrest made at the conclusion of a *formal investigation* will likely have more supplementary pages and the arrest cover page is submitted after the G.O.R. is written. If the arrest is made at the crime scene or during the *preliminary investigation*, the arrest cover page is submitted instead of a G.O.R. cover page. Both cover pages are the same except for the heading and the specific arrest information.

5

Arrest Report

Circumstances that constitute an arrest or detention, by definition, require an *arrest report*.

Arrest is defined as:
(i)   actual restraint on a person's liberty, against that person's will; or
(ii)   physical custody of a person with the intent to detain.

Detention is defined by the Supreme Court of Canada, in *R.v. Therens (1985) 18 C.C.C.(3d) p.481 (S.C.C.)*, as;
(i)   deprivation of liberty by physical constraint; or
(ii)   the assuming of control over the movement of a person by demand or direction of a police officer; or
(iii) a psychological compulsion existing within a person in the form of a perception that his/her freedom has been removed.

An arrest report is composed of a **cover page** and a **narrative**.

The **cover page** is the same as the one used for the G.O.R. In addition to the same information, the arresting officer must state the:
- *accused person's personal information* (name, address, date of birth, description)
- *names of offences* that the accused person committed,
- the *time of arrest*,
- the *time of release*,
- the *method of release*.

The accuracy of the *times* are crucial in case any aspect of the arrest/detention is questioned for validity.

Arrests that result in an *unconditional release* (no charges laid) must be documented by means of an arrest report. An unconditional release does not cancel the fact that an arrest or detention occurred.

The **narrative principles** are the same as those used for a G.O.R. The narrative must justify the arrest or detention. Consequently, sufficient evidence must exist in the narrative that:
- *explains the officer's observations, if the officer found the offence **being committed**. Officers are required to explain a variety of offences that are commonly witnessed. For example, officers see persons **assault** others, they see people **steal** and **damage** property and they see people who are **intoxicated**. Paraphrasing detracts from written proof that certain facts*

*in issue existed. Opinions are acceptable only if they summarize an observation, after the observation has been described. Merely stating that a person was **intoxicated** is insufficient. Describe the physical condition first, then state an opinion of degree of intoxication.*

- *precisely describes the **reasonable grounds** that the arrest was* predicated upon, if the offence was indictable or dual procedure.

An arrest is made during one of two time periods:

- by the uniform patrol officer, at or near the crime scene, during the *preliminary investigation*, or
- by the C.I.B. Officer, at the conclusion of a *formal investigation.*

Example: Impaired Driving - Arrest Report and Summary

This charge arises from an incident which occurred on 94-01-06 at 22:00 hrs. on King Street in the city of Welland.

The accused person in this matter is Gord Clemens, d.o.b. 40-11-20, 5000 Main Street, Welland.

On 94-01-06 at 22:00 hrs. the accused person was operating a 1986 Pontiac Sunbird, bearing Ontario registration NET 199 northbound on King Street in Welland. No other occupants were in the vehicle. The vehicle was travelling at 70 km/hr. The maximum posted speed on King Street is 50 km/hr. The vehicle twice weaved partially into the southbound lane of traffic.

Cst. Friendly was following the accused person's vehicle at a distance of about 10 meters. Nothing obstructed Cst. Friendly's view. The officer followed the accused from Ontario Road to King Street, a distance of approximately 300 metres, for a duration of about 15 seconds.

Cst. Friendly activated the roof lights of the vehicle and the accused person stopped immediately. The officer walked to the driver's window and spoke to the accused person. Cst. Friendly asked the accused to produce his driver's licence, ownership and insurance. The accused made no verbal response and removed a wallet from his back pocket. The accused searched through the wallet and repeatedly passed over the driver's licence without recognizing it.

The accused's breath smelled of an alcoholic beverage and his eyes were bloodshot. Cst. Friendly told the accused to exit the vehicle. The accused's verbal response was incoherent because his speech was slurred. The accused opened the driver's door, and fell to the ground as he stepped out. The accused stood up and Cst. Friendly arrested him for Impaired Driving. The accused was informed of his right to counsel and a Breathalyzer demand was read to him. The accused was cautioned and was subsequently transported to the police station.

At 22:20 hrs., the accused supplied a sample of breath to a qualified technician. The Breathalyzer reading indicated a blood alcohol concentration of 250 mgs. At 22:35 hrs., a second breath sample was provided indicating the same blood alcohol concentration.

The accused was later released by means of a Promise to Appear.

6

Witness Statement

Witness statements are formal, written records of a witness's observations, perceived by his/her own senses, that explain precisely the verbal evidence that he/she may be capable of testifying about in court.

The statement itself does *not* represent documentary or physical evidence that will be admitted in court to replace the witness's verbal testimony. The police officer who wrote the statement cannot read it during the trial, this would constitute **hearsay** evidence. This is permitted at other judicial proceedings, such as *ex parte hearings* and *bail hearings*. Essentially, a witness statement explains the verbal evidence that the witness *will say* at the trial.

Additionally, witness statements may be used by the witness to refresh his or her memory before the trial. A witness may read his or her statement if the statement was *contemporaneous*, meaning that:

1. The witness read the statement at the time it was dictated to the police and the witness signed it, and
2. The statement was taken shortly after the observation was made by the witness.

Purpose: Witness statements serve the following purposes:

1. Instructions to the Crown Attorney conveying the potential evidence that the witness may testify about.
2. Written record of *reasonable grounds* justifying an officer's actions.
3. A documented record to aid the officer's memory.
4. A legal remedy for a *hostile* or *adverse witness*:

General Principles:

1. Written in the first person
2. Witness's own perceptions
3. No hearsay evidence
4. Sequenced, structured and specific; not general or vague

Procedure: Witnesses should always dictate their observations and officers should write the statement. Witnesses should not be allowed to write their own statements to prevent relevant information from being neglected because a witness does not know what information is relevant to the facts in issue of a specific offence.

Statements are divided in the following parts, including the information required for each part:

1. **Heading** - The witness' name followed by "will say" is the usual heading - e.g., "June Clemen will say:" Another type of heading used is "The anticipated evidence of June Clemen." The statement then follows in the *first person*, that is, as though the witness is telling the story, i.e., I am, I saw.

2.   **Introduction** - The witness introduces him/herself by means of a current personal resumé that includes:
- age
- address
- marital status
- number of children
- occupation, place of employment and position held. If no occupation, state the witnesses specific status, i.e., welfare recipient, disability pension, etc.

3.   **Events before the offence -** The witness's activities preceding his or her observations of the offence are recorded here. Facts may include:
- day, date
- work hours
- visits, socializing, alcohol or drug consumption
- witness's physical condition - sober, had been drinking or intoxicated. Describe the intoxicated condition rather than araphrasing and concluding that the suspect was intoxicated
- relevant communication with the offender, including *verbatim conversation*, which may corroborate *mens rea*
- offender's identity, description
- whether the offender is *known* or *unknown* to the witness
- witness's capability of facially recognizing offender in the future.
- factors affecting observation (i.e., intent to learn)
- hearsay evidence

4.   **Events During the Offence -** Observations relating to the **actus reus** (the physical act) of the offence are recorded here. Principles include:
- time observation began
- description of each act relating to the *facts in issue.*
- *avoid* generalizations that use the words *assault, threaten* or *stole*. Describe the act instead.
- *verbatim* statements made by offender
- identity of offender, if known, including description
- describe suspect, if identity is unknown
- capability of facial recognition
- *factors affecting observation*

5.   **Events After the Offence -** Observation relating to the witness's activities after the commission of the offence concluded are recorded here. Principles include:
- relevant acts by the offender that corroborate *mens rea* and any *facts in issue.* For example, possession and disposal of stolen property, weapons or any physical evidence.
- any communication with the offender. All conversation should be recorded **verbatim**.
- any significant events that may have affected the witness's recall between the time of observation and the time of the interview.

At the conclusion of the statement:
- have the witness read it
- if mistakes exist, have the witness delete unwanted errors by drawing a single line through them and initialling the change, or, add any corrections and have the witness initial them
- ensure that the witness signs or initials the bottom of each page, following the last word, and signs the last page with his or her usual signature, after the last word
- the officer should witness the signatures.

Additionally, the officer should record the following information in his or her notebook:
- *time* interview commenced
- *time* interview concluded
- *location* of interview
- *presence* of any other persons.

Examples:
Attempt Break and Enter - Witness Statement (suspect known)
(Improper Format)

> June Doe will say:
>   I am forty-five years of age. I live at 10 King Street, Apt. 6 with my husband Bill. I am employed as a court clerk for Provincial Court - Family Division.
>   On November 6, 1993, I was at home with my husband. We were watching TV. at about 9:00 p.m., I heard people screaming in the hallway of our floor. I heard a voice say, "Move out of here. Go back to where you came from." Then someone started banging on the door. I heard more yelling, such as, "Did you hear me? Move out, go back to your own country." I heard him turning the door knob trying to get into the apartment. I feared for my safety as well as my husband's. We had been living in fear for about one month. We've been threatened to move and we've had damage caused to our car. The people in the apartment across the hall have been harassing and threatening us for the past month. I called the police and officers arrived within minutes. I spoke to an officer in the doorway of my apartment and I reported this incident to him. The other officer was speaking to the people in the apartment across from ours. The tenant started threatening us and the officer arrested him.
>
> signed, June Doe
> 9:30 p.m. Nov. 6, 1993

The previous statement lacks sufficiency regarding:
1. Identity and recognition of the offender;
2. Proof of the facts in issue of the offence, "Attempted Break and Enter";
3. Specificity of certain acts relative to mens rea; and
4. Order of events: before, during and after the offence.

(Proper Format)

> June Doe will say: (or, the anticipated evidence of June Doe:)
>   I am forty-five years of age. My husband Bill and I have been legally married for twenty years. We have no children. We immigrated to Canada from Asia, twenty years ago. We are the tenants of 10 King Street, Apt. #6 in (city). I am employed by Provincial Court - Family Division, where I hold the position of court clerk.
>   Bill and I moved to our current apartment on October 1, 1993. A man named Eddie Ton lives in Apt. #5 with his wife. Their apartment is across the hall from ours. Eddie is a white male, twenty-five years old; 6'1"; average build; shoulder length, dark hair parted in the middle; dark moustache. I know his name because I checked his mailbox. I have seen him on numerous occasions during the past month.

(Proper Format) (con't)

Sometime during the first week of October, I parked my car in the back parking lot at about 6:00 p.m. Eddie was in the parking lot, standing about 30 feet from me. He made a racist remark and said, "Go back to your own country." About three or four days later, in the evening, Bill and I were in our apartment. A loud party was in progress in Eddie's apartment. I heard a man yelling racist remarks about our Asian descent. The man was in the hallway. I opened our door slightly and saw Eddie in the hallway. He said, "Move out of here or we'll burn your car with you in it."

Sometime during the middle of October, I found a racist remark scratched on the side of my car.

About one week ago, at 10:00 p.m., I heard banging on the door. I heard a man's voice, which I believed to be Eddie's, yelling racist remarks.

On November 6, 1993, I worked the 9 a.m. - 5 p.m. shift. Bill worked similar hours. We arrived home at about 5:30 p.m. We ate supper at 6:00 p.m. We consumed no alcohol. At 7:00 p.m. we sat in our living room and watched TV. The entrance to our apartment is about 10 feet from the livingroom. I locked the door at that time.

At about 9:00 p.m. I heard people screaming in the hallway. Bill and I were watching TV. I heard a man's voice, which I recognized as Eddie's, yelling, "Move out of here. Go back where you came from." I heard banging on our door shortly afterward. I heard the same voice yelling, "Did you hear me? Move out, go back to your own country." I heard the door knob being moved. I saw it moving back and forth repeatedly. I looked out the peephole on the door. I saw Eddie standing alone in the hallway. I heard more banging on the door. I immediately phoned the police.

Officers arrived a few minutes later. As I reported this incident to one officer with our door open, I saw the other officer speaking to Eddie in his apartment. Eddie was seated at a table. His wife and two other men were also seated there. I was about 20 feet from them.

Eddie got up and walked toward me saying, "You want trouble?". The officer arrested him and removed him from the building.

signed June Doe
9:30 p.m. Nov. 6, 1993

Domestic Assault - Witness Statement (suspect known)

June Doe will say: (or, the anticipated evidence of June Doe:)

I am thirty-two years old. I live at 10 Main Street in (city), with my husband Bill. We have been legally married for twelve years and we have two sons, Wally age 10, and Timothy, age 5. I am employed at the First National Bank where I hold the position of manager.

On Monday, October 1, 1991. I woke up at 6:30 a.m. I was scheduled to work the 9 a.m.- 5 p.m. shift. Bill was scheduled to work the same hours. We ate breakfast together. Casual conversation occurred. No arguments or hostility existed.

I left home at 8:30 a.m. and arrived at work at 8:45 a.m. My morning schedule was very busy. I met a client at a restaurant at 12:15 p.m. for lunch. I consumed no alcohol. At 1:10 p.m. I returned to work.

Domestic Assault - Witness Statement (con't)

Bill phoned me at 2:05 p.m. and the following conversation occurred:
>   Bill: What are you doing?
>   June: I'm busy.
>   Bill: I lost out on another promotion.
>   June: Have you been drinking again?
>   Bill: Ya, get off my back. I only had a couple of beers at lunch.
>   June: I'm busy; I'll talk to you tonight.

I hung up the phone even though I could still hear Bill talking. I left the bank at 5:20 p.m. I drove to The Grocery Store, situated at 111 King Street. I purchased groceries at 5:30 and left at 5:45 p.m. At 6:00 p.m. I arrived home. I made no other stops. I entered the house through the back door and put the groceries away. Timothy was sitting at the kitchen table with a colouring book.

The TV was on in the living room. The living room is situated adjacent to the kitchen. The rooms are separated by a wall. There is a 3' x 3' opening in this wall. It is situated above the kitchen sink.

Our L-shaped couch is situated in the living room beneath the opening.

I looked into the living room and saw Wally and Bill sitting on the couch. Bill was seated with his back to me, directly beneath the opening. Three empty beer bottles were on the living room floor about two feet from Bill. The labels had been removed. Bill was holding a beer bottle in his right hand. I couldn't see if beer was in it. The following conversation occurred:
>   Bill: It's about time you got home. Are we eating soon?
>   June: Ya.
>   Bill: I got to get the next promotion.

At 6:05 p.m. Bill appeared in the kitchen entrance. He walked to the refrigerator and opened it. The following conversation occurred;
>   Bill: Are we out of beer?
>   June: How should I know? Haven't you had enough?

I was standing about two feet from him. Bill turned to face me and said, 'How would you like a smack? You're asking for it." I said. "Go lay down. You need help."

He raised his right arm, his fist was clenched and he struck my nose with his fist.

I walked to a wall phone in the kitchen. I dialled the police number while Bill said. "Put that down or you're dead." He walked out of the kitchen toward the living room. He had a full bottle of beer in his hands.

I asked the police dispatcher for an officer to come. My nose was bleeding. I held a towel to it. I went to the front door to wait. The officer arrived at 6:10 p.m. I did not see or converse with Bill.

I told the officer this story. He went into the living room while I went outside with the children. About one minute later, Bill was being escorted by the officer to a police vehicle parked in the driveway. Both entered the police vehicle, they left at 6:20 p.m.

I drove to the hospital accompanied by the kids. I had the same towel with me. I arrived at the hospital at 6:30 p.m. Dr. Smith examined me at 6:40 p.m. I returned home at 7:00 p.m.

The officer was present. I gave him the towel and dictated a statement to him.

Impaired Driving - Witness Statement (suspect known)

Cst. Friendly will say:

I am a member of the Niagara Regional Police Force, where I hold the rank of Constable. I am assigned to the uniform branch of number 33 division, in the city of Welland.

On January 6, 1994, I was working the 7:00 p.m. to 7:00 a.m. shift, assigned to general patrol duties.

At 10:00 p.m., I was parked at the corner of King Street and Ontario Street, in the city of Welland, in a parking lot situated at the north east corner of the intersection. At that time I saw a grey vehicle driving northbound on King Street. King Street has a maximum speed of 50 km/hr. The vehicle appeared to be travelling at an excessive speed. I drove onto King Street and followed this vehicle. No cars were between my police vehicle and this vehicle. Visibility was clear. As I approached the vehicle at a distance of approximately 10 meters, I saw the car drive into the southbound lane and return into the northbound lane. Seconds later, the vehicle again drove into the southbound lane and returned to the northbound lane. I looked at my speedometer. It indicated that my police vehicle was travelling at a speed of 70 km/hr. The distance between my police vehicle and the vehicle remained the same. I activated my roof lights. The car immediately stopped along the right curb. The plate number of the car was NET 199, Ontario.

I walked to the driver's window and a male person was seated in the driver's seat. No other occupants were in the car. The male person was about 40 years of age, had short brown hair and was clean shaven. I immediately detected an odour of alcohol on his breath. I saw that his eyes were bloodshot. The following conversation occurred:

CF: Can I see your driver's licence, ownership and insurance?

BC: (no response)

The accused reached into his right back pocket and removed a black wallet. He opened it while holding it on his lap and began searching through it. I saw a driver's licence three times as he searched through documents but the accused did not take the driver's licence out of his wallet. I asked the accused, "Could you step out of the car?" The accused made a response that I could not understand. The accused opened the driver's door, stepped out and fell to the ground.

I took hold of his right arm and helped the accused stand up. I reached down and picked up his wallet for him. In my opinion, the accused was intoxicated. I said to him, "You are under arrest for Impaired Driving. It is my duty to inform you that you have the right to retain and instruct counsel without delay. Do you understand?" The accused responded, "Yes." I told him, "Legal aid exists and is available. Do you understand?" The accused responded, "Yes". I told him, "You have to come to the police station and take a Breathalyzer test. If you refuse to take it you can be charged under the Criminal Code. Do you understand?". The accused replied, "Ya."

We walked to the police vehicle while I held his right arm. The accused had poor balance and could not walk straight. He was seated in the back of the police vhicle. After I entered the front of the police vehicle I stated the following to

Impaired Driving - Witness Statement (con't)

him, "Do you wish to say anything in answer to the charge ? You are not obliged to say anything unless you wish to do so, but whatever you say may be given in evidence. Do you understand?" The accused responded, "Ya."

The following conversation occurred before we left the scene:

CF: What is your name?
BC: Bill
CF: Bill what?
BC: Clemen
CF: Can you spell that?
BC: C-L-E-M-E-N
CF: What is your date of birth?
BC: November 20, 1940
CF: How much have you had to drink tonight?
BC: Lots

We left the scene at 10:07 p.m. and arrived at the Welland Police Station at 10:12 p.m. I escorted the accused person through the security garage into the Breathalyser room.

The accused remained seated in the room until 10:15 p.m. At that time I introduced him to Cst. Smith.

signed Cst. Friendly
10:30 p.m. January 6, 1994

7

Crown Brief

A **Crown Brief** is a written document, of varied lengths, that explains all the facts, circumstances and evidence of an offence for the purpose of prosecuting the accused person(s) in the matter.

A Crown Brief is prepared only after an information has been laid to formally charge an accused person(s). Conversely, a Crown Brief is not required if no charges are laid regarding an occurrence.

Crown briefs are prepared by the police. Usually the officer in charge of the case (investigator) is assigned the responsibility of writing it. After it is completed, the Crown Brief is submitted to the Crown Attorney, who retains possession of it until the trial. The Crown Attorney uses the Crown Brief during the preparation of the prosecution and during the trial. Therefore, Crown Briefs are a police officer's *primary means of communicating* the evidence that has been obtained during an investigation to the Crown Attorney. Consequently, the success of a prosecution is largely dependent upon the thoroughness, relevancy and accuracy of the Crown Brief prepared by the officer.

Additionally, the Crown Brief is the Crown Attorney's *primary means* of *making disclosure* to the defence/accused person. The Crown has the onus to provide disclosure to the accused after an information has been laid. Failure to provide disclosure may constitute a section 7 Charter violation. Therefore, *an incomplete Crown Brief may be equivalent to improper disclosure, that may result in a Charter violation.*

Principles: The principles of preparing a Crown Brief should fulfill the Supreme Court of Canada's guidelines relating to proper disclosure, found in *R.v. Stinchcombe (1991) 68 C.C.C. (3d) p.91 (S.C.C.).*

Disclosure is defined as the divulging of *all relevant material* by the Crown to the accused/ defence, after an information has been laid. A Crown Brief must contain *all relevant material* because the Crown Brief is the primary means of providing disclosure.

Relevant material is defined as:
- any information that is of "some use". The defence determines what information is of some use, not the Crown.
- inculpatory and exculpatory evidence. Evidence obtained by the police that benefits the defence cannot be concealed by the Crown.
- all statements obtained from persons by police officers, whether or not the person will be compelled to court by the Crown as a witness. The statement of a person who will not be subpoenaed by the Crown cannot be concealed by the Crown.

- name, address and occupation of persons from whom *no* statement was taken. If the person was interviewed by an officer and the person's observations were recorded in the officer's notebook, the officer's notes must be disclosed. The only exception is the identity of a confidential informant; how ever, this exception is subject to review by the trial judge.

Initial disclosure should be made before the accused enters a plea. Consequently, the Crown Brief must be submitted to the defence before the accused's first appearance in court.

The Crown's obligation of disclosure does not end after the initial disclosing of the Crown Brief. After the initial Crown Brief is submitted to the defence, all relevant material obtained by the police, must be disclosed to the defence also. The Crown cannot conceal any evidence obtained **after** the information is sworn and the Crown Brief is prepared because the Crown's disclosure obligation is a continuous one until the trial. Therefore, Crown Briefs must be added to whenever additional evidence is obtained.

Procedure: A Crown Brief is composed of the following parts:
- cover page
- introduction page
- witness list
- summary
- witness statements

Cover Page - The title of the case is the only information typed on this page.

Example # 14:

> Regina
> vs.
> [Name of accused person(s)]

Introduction Page - Basic information relating to the case is written here.

Example #15:

OFFENCE:	- short form name of offence (e.g., Robbery)
	- section number and statute
	(e.g., sec.344 Criminal Code of Canada)
DATE:	April 25, 1993
ACCUSED:	Eddie Herron
	1000 King Street,
	Welland, Ontario
	D.O.B. 1969-Aug.-02
PLACE:	City of Welland
OFFICER IN CHARGE:	Cst. Friendly

Witness List - All witnesses that will be subpoenaed by the Crown must be listed including, sufficient information to find them and serve them with a subpoena - i.e. name, home address and work address.

The officer must list enough witnesses to prove each *fact in issue* of the offence beyond reasonable doubt. A *synopsis* that briefly describes the witness's position and what evidence they have to give may be printed next to the witness's name.

Example #16:

WITNESS LIST	SYNOPSIS
1. Mary Feld 1000 King St. Welland, Ont. or c/o First National Bank 2000 Main St., Welland, Ont.	-bank manager -witnessed robbery
2. Barb Smith 5000 Rice Rd. Welland, Ont. or c/o First National Bank 2000 Main St., Welland, Ont.	- bank teller; had gun - pointed at her and was robbed of money

Summary - The **summary** is a narrative that explains, beyond a reasonable doubt, that the accused person committed the offence alleged in the information.

In cases where the accused enters a guilty plea, the summary represents the Crown Attorney's *primary means of communication* to the trial judge.

If the accused enters a guilty plea, the Crown Attorney reads the summary to the trial judge. Consequently, a summary must fulfill the following *principles*:

(i)   a summary must unequivocally establish a *prima facie case*
(ii)   a summary must prove all the *facts in issue* of the offence, beyond reasonable doubt.

Consequently, the officer writing the summary must know the *facts in issue* that compose the offence that the accused person is charged with, stated in the information. Therefore, the summary must include:

- the constant facts in issue
  - identity of accused
  - date & time of offence
  - location of offence
- the facts in issue that compose the *actus reus*. These are determined by analysis of the relevant section where the offence is found.
- *mens rea*

Format: A summary should be written in four phases:

(i)   introduction
(ii)   events before the offence
(iii) events during the offence
(iv)   events after the offence

(i) **Introduction**. In this phase, the writer should state who the *complainant/victim* is, who the *accused person* is, *when* the offence occurred and *where* it occurred.

Example #17:

> The charge of robbery in this matter arises from an incident which occurred at the First National Bank, situated at 2000 Main Street in the city of Welland, Ontario, on Tuesday, April 25, 1993.
>   The accused person charged with robbery in this matter is:
>   Eddie Herron, D.O.B. 1969 Aug. 02,
>   10000 Rice Rd., Welland.
>
> The circumstances of the offence are as follows:

(ii) **Events Before the Offence**. This phase includes relevant evidence that helps prove any fact in issue that occurred before the commission of the offence.

Example #18:

> On Tuesday, April 25, 1993, the bank opened for business at 09:00 hrs. Fourteen employees worked that day.
>   At about 15:00 hrs., Herron entered the bank via the front door. He disguised himself by wearing a black nylon stocking over his head. He had possession of a .38 calibre Smith and Wesson handgun.
>   Wilma Samson, a bank teller, was assigned wicket #4.

The relevant facts explained in this phase were:
- date, time & place
- the bank was open for business
- number of employees
- disguise & the weapon
- the position of the victim

All of the previous facts are relevant to the facts in issue pertaining to the offence of "robbery".

(iii) **Events During the Offence**. This phase describes the actus reus that constitutes the offence. The prominent *principles* to follow are:
- avoid using the name of the offence to describe the offender's action. For example, do not state, "The accused then *robbed* the teller ..." Replace the offence name with precise explanation of the physical acts.
- the writer must be cognizant of the *facts in issue* that compose the offence. This narrative must directly be relevant to those facts in issue.
- use verbatim quotations to describe accused's verbal statements. Do not paraphrase.

Example # 19:

> Herron walked to wicket #4 and pointed the handgun at Mrs. Samson's head, saying, "Give me all your money."
>   Mrs. Samson complied by removing $8000.00 from the wicket drawer, placing the cash into a canvas bag and giving the bag to Herron. Herron took possession of the canvas bag and ran out the front entrance.

(iv) **Events After the Offence**. This phase includes circumstances that prove the facts in issue which occurred *after the actus reus concluded*. The following principles are applicable to this narrative:

- include any facts that incriminate the accused.
- include the disposal and recovery of physical evidence
- state the date & time of arrest and when the accused was informed of the right to counsel
- state whether or not the accused gave a confession to police
- indicate if accused gave a written confession. The contents of the statement do not have to be included in the summary. Instead, the confession should be attached to the summary.

Example #20:

> Herron ran toward a parking lot situated at the rear of the bank, by using an alley along the west wall of the bank. He entered a parked 1980 Mazda, bearing Ontario Registration 123-ABC.
>
> The police were contacted and an investigation began.
>
> On April 26, 1993, two $10.00 bills were recovered from a business premises in Welland. The money was identified as having been stolen from the bank. Herron was identified as having been the possessor of the money.
>
> On April 27, 1993, Herron was identified by a witness who saw him enter the bank after he placed the stocking over his head.
>
> A Criminal Code search warrant was later executed at Herron's house. A handgun, a black nylon mask and a canvas bag were recovered. The canvas bag contained $7,980.00
>
> Herron was arrested on April 27, 1993, for this robbery. He was informed of his right to counsel and was cautioned. He was transported to the Welland police station and was interrogated. Herron gave a written confession to police.
>
> A bail hearing was conducted. Herron was released by means of an undertaking with conditions.

Witness Statements: The majority of a Crown Brief is composed of witness statements. All statements are written in the format discussed in Section 5.

The witness statements must reflect the required evidence to prove the circumstances written in the summary. In other words, the combined witness statements must constitute a *prima facie* case.

Example: *Crown Brief (pages 38-44)*

Regina

vs.

Wally Beaulieu
Clarence Ruffington
Eddie Herron

OFFENCE: ROBBERY,
                                SECTION 344, CRIMINAL CODE OF CANADA.

DATE: JANUARY 10, 1994.

ACCUSED: (1)   Wally BEAULIEU
                                   1000 King Street,
                                   WELLAND, Ontario

                                   d.o.b. (1972 February 05)

                            (2)   Clarence RUFFINGTON
                                   3000 Lincoln Street,
                                   WELLAND, Ontario

                                   d.o.b. (1969 May 25)

                            (3)   Eddie HERRON
                                   800 East Main Street
                                   WELLAND, Ontario

                                   d.o.b. (1969 October 12)

PLACE: CITY OF WELLAND

OFFICER: CST. FRIENDLY

| WITNESSES | SYNOPSIS |

(1)	JUNE MARTINO 8000 Woodlawn Rd. Welland, Ontario or	- witness outside bank; saw suspects prior to and after robbery.
c/o	The High School 1 Pelham Street Welland, Ontario	
(2)	ALLEN O'NEILL 1000 Clare Avenue Welland, Ontario or	- witnessed plate number of suspect vehicle.
c/o	Jerry's Construction Centre Street Welland, Ontario	
(3)	WILMA SAMSON 5000 Sugarloaf St. Port Colborne, Ontario or	- bank teller; had gun pointed at her and robbed of money.
c/o	National Bank 1500 East Main Street Welland, Ontario	
(4)	SUSAN JONES 7000 First Avenue Welland, Ontario or	- bank employee; had knife held to her throat.
c/o	National Bank 1500 East Main Street Welland, Ontario	
(5)	BARB SMITH 9000 Sumbler Road Welland, Ontario or	- bank teller; had knife pointed at her and was robbed of money.
c/o	National Bank 1500 East Main Street Welland, Ontario	

SUMMARY:

The charges of robbery in this matter arise from an incident which occurred at the National Bank, situated at 1500 East Main Street, in the city of Welland, on January 10, 1994.

The three persons charged with robbery in this matter are:

    1. Wally BEAULIEU, d.o.b. 72-FEB-05, 1000 King St., Welland

    2. Clarence RUFFINGTON, d.o.b.. 69-MAY-25, 3000 Lincoln St., Welland

    3. Eddie HERRON , d.o.b. 69-OCT-12, 800 East Main St., Welland

The circumstances of the offence are as follows:

At about 3:00 p.m., BEAULIEU and RUFFINGTON entered the bank via the front entrance while HERRON remained in a van parked behind the bank. The bank was open for business at the time.

Both wore black nylon stockings over their heads; BEAULIEU was armed with a knife and RUFFINGTON was armed with a handgun. They went to a counter where the bank teller, Wilma SAMSON, was working. Mrs. SAMSON had been waiting on a customer. RUFFINGTON pushed the customer who was positioned at the counter, and he confronted Mrs. SAMSON. RUFFINGTON held the gun through the wicket, pointed it at Mrs. SAMSON and demanded money.

BEAULIEU went to the counter near the wicket area where Mrs. SMITH was working. A bank employee, Susan JONES, was standing near this area. BEAULIEU put his arm around JONES's neck and held the knife in front of her face. BEAULIEU shoved JONES, pointed the knife at her, and instructed her to move away toward a wall. Subsequently, BEAULIEU pointed the knife to Mrs. SMITH and jabbed it toward her as he demanded money.

Both tellers complied and gave BEAULIEU and RUFFINGTON cash from the teller's drawers. The money was placed in a bag, the accused persons took possession of the cash, and they fled from the bank.

The total amount of money stolen from the bank was $9,000.00. Included in that amount were twenty, ten dollar bills, whose serial numbers had been previously recorded by the bank.

BEAULIEU and RUFFINGTON ran north in an alley which is adjacent to the bank, and met HERRON who was sitting in a van, bearing Ontario registration 123-ABC, in the Cross Street parking lot. Subsequently they entered the van and drove from the scene. The Niagara Regional Police Force was contacted and an investigation commenced.

On January 11, 1994, two $10.00 bills were recovered from a business premise in Grimsby, Ontario. The money was identified as having been stolen from the National Bank.

As a result of further investigation, HERRON was arrested on January 12, 1994. He was cautioned and informed of his right to counsel. During questioning, he verbally admitted to C.I.B. Officers that he participated in this incident.

BEAULIEU and RUFFINGTON were arrested on January 15, 1994. Both were cautioned and informed of their right to counsel.

During questioning, BEAULIEU admitted that he participated in this offence and gave a written confession to C.I.B. Officers. RUFFINGTON verbally admitted that he participated in the offence and explained to C.I.B. Officers that he had used a .38 calibre revolver during the commission of the robbery.

Only $20.00 was recovered.

BEAULIEU was released by means of an undertaking. HERRON was held in custody following a bail hearing. RUFFINGTON was held in custody pending a bail hearing.

Note to reader: Witness statements follow next. In an actual "Crown Brief", each witness statement would occupy its own page(s); they would not run together as illustrated on pages 42-44 in this publication.

ALLEN O'NEILL WILL SAY:
    I am 21 years old. I live at 1000 Clare Avenue, Welland. I work at Jerry's Construction, Centre Street, Welland.
    On Monday, January 10, 1994, I worked from 7 a.m. to 3 p.m. at Jerry's Construction. At about 2:55 p.m., I left work and I was driving my motorcycle. I was on my way home driving down East Main Street. As I passed the National Bank, I saw one guy running into the alley next to the bank. He was holding a bag that you see in the bank. He was wearing a black stocking over his head. The guy ran north down the alley. I can't remember anything else he was wearing.
    I turned right onto the last street near the canal. At the end of the street, I saw a white van driving past JIM's GYM toward Cross Street. I saw the back of the van. I didn't see any other vehicles moving. I followed the van to Main Street. I read the plate at that corner and the plate was 123 ABC. It could probably be a Chevy van, late 70's, no side window. I pulled to the right of the van. I took a very fast look and I'm pretty sure I saw only the driver who looked like a young male. I drove around the block again and I went home. As soon as I got in my house I wrote down the plate number. It took me about 4 minutes to get home after I read the plate.
    At 7:50 p.m. I went to the Welland Police Station and I gave the piece of paper to Cst. Friendly.

signed Allen O'Neill
January 10, 1994
7:40 p.m.

JUNE MARTINO WILL SAY:
    I am 15 years old. I live at 8000 Woodlawn Road, Welland. I am a grade 9 student at The High school in Welland.
    On Monday, January 10, 1994, my mother picked me up at school at about 1:30 p.m. We drove to East Main Street, Welland. We arrived at 2:45 pm. and parked in front of the National Bank, 1500 East Main Street, Welland. We parked along the north curb, in front of the restaurant next door. I was sitting in the front passenger seat. My mother left the car and I stayed inside the car, alone, for about 5 minutes. During that time I saw a man standing on the sidewalk in front of the alley next to the bank. He had his hands in his pocket and was looking at me. I can describe him as follows: male/white, 19 years, 5'6" chubby, short dirty blonde hair, clean shaven, bad acne on his face; wearing a one piece gas station attendant suit, blue in colour. The suit had a little sign on the front but I could not read it. The suit looks the same as the ones worn at a gas station on East Main Street, across the street from The Social Club. I can show the gas station to the police. I've been with my mother at that gas station and I'm pretty sure the people there wear the same kind. I would be able to recognize this person if I saw him again.
    A second man walked up to #1. The second man came from the alley to meet him. #2 is described as follows: male/white; 6' skinny, short straight brown hair, some facial hair (stubble) and a moustache (thin); heavy knit, crew neck burgundy sweater, black jeans, brown work boots (old).
    They both looked at me again. They walked to the front door of the bank and stood outside for a moment. #1, the short man, put black panty hose over his head. #2, the taller one, also put black panty hose over his head. I did not see any weapons at this time.
    Both went in the bank and I stayed in the car. They were in the bank for about 4 minutes. They then came out of the bank, both were running. #2 (tall man) was holding a bank bag. The other man (#1, short man) was holding a knife and a gun. The knife had a blade about 12" long and a brown handle; it looked like a jackknife.. The gun was brown and looked fake. The barrel was very short. Both men ran to the alley, and ran north, down the alley, along the side of the bank.

signed June Martino
January 10, 1994
3:40 p.m.

WILMA SAMSON WILL SAY:

My name is Wilma SAMSON, I am 31 years old and I live at 5000 Sugarloaf St., Port Colborne with my husband and two children.

I work as a part-time teller at National Bank at 1500 East Main Street, Welland. I have worked there for 2 years.

On January 10, 1993 I was working at the National Bank from 9 a.m. to 5 p.m. At approximately 3:00 p.m., I was at my wicket and I was waiting on a customer.

I then heard yelling. I looked up. The customer was being pushed out of the way by a man.

The man was wearing a black nylon mask over his head. He was approximately 6' tall, 170 lbs. and may have had light brown hair. He was wearing something blue and may have been in his early 20's. There was a second man that also entered the bank and was wearing a black nylon stocking over his head. The second man did not come to my wicket. He was shorter (approx. 5'6") and looked to be in his 30's.

The first man, who pushed my customer out of the way, came up to my counter and pointed a gun at me in between the wicket. He then said, "Gimme the money now!" He kept jabbing the gun toward me and moving it up and down.

I started to take all the money out of my top drawer which contained my $10.00 and $20.00 bills. The man then yelled, "No not that, the bottom drawer, the large stuff!!" I gave him the money in the bottom drawer. While I did that, he kept saying," Give me more, I want it all." Within the money that I gave him was the "bait" money that the bank keeps a record of the serial numbers so the money is traceable. The "bait" money I gave him consisted of 10 - $10.00 bills.

He kept yelling for more money so I began to gather my $5.00 and $2.00 bills, but he ran out of the bank without taking them. The other man who had been at another wicket also ran out of the bank at the same time he did. The one that was at my wicket took approximately $4000.00 in total.

signed Wilma Samson
January 10, 1994
4:05 p.m.

SUSAN JONES WILL SAY:

My name is Susan Jones. I am 46 years old and I live at 7000 First Ave., Welland with my husband. I am the assistant manager of Commercial Credit at the National Bank at 1500 East Main Street, Welland. I have been employed by this bank for seven years.

On Monday, January 10, 1994, I was working at the National Bank located at 1500 East Main Street, Welland. At approximately 3:00 p.m. I was in the main lobby of the bank, standing by Barb Smith's wicket talking to a customer.

All of a sudden, someone put their arm around my neck and held a knife in front of my face with their left hand. The person who was holding me then turned me towards the front door and I saw another man run into the bank. He was wearing a black nylon stocking over his head and was holding a handgun that seemed to have a long barrel.

The man who was holding me then shoved me away from him and pointed the knife at me and said, "Get back against the wall, move it!" He jabbed the knife toward me and then pointed it toward the teller, Barb Smith.

I stayed against the wall and just watched him. He demanded money from Barb Smith and she gathered it for him. He was 25-30 years old. He was around 5'10" or 5'11" tall and weighed approximately 150 lbs. He had on a black nylon stocking over his head. It looked like he had sandy blond or light brown hair. His lips were skinny and his teeth were rotten on the left hand side, on the top. He was wearing light blue jeans that were faded from washing. He had on black vinyl runners with a name on the side that I could not see. He had on a brown/olive coloured shaker knit sweater on.

The knife was a hunting knife, about 10" long. It had a wide silver blade that was slightly curved at the end.

Once Barb gave him all the money he picked it up and then ran out with the other man that had also entered the bank in a black nylon stocking mask.

I then ran to the door to see which way they were going, but they were already out of sight. A customer that was outside the door, just coming into the bank said that they had ran down the alley.

signed Susan Jones
Monday, January 10, 1994
4:15 p.m.

BARB SMITH WILL SAY:

I am 29 years old and I live at 9000 Sumbler Road, Welland with my husband and my daughter. I work at the National Bank, 1500 East Main Street, Welland. I have been employed there for 9 years.

On Monday, January 10, 1994, I was working from 9 a.m. - 5 p.m. At approximately 3:05 p.m. or 3:10 p.m., I was looking down into my cash drawer when I heard a commotion right in front of my wicket. As I looked up I saw a guy with a black ladies stocking over his head. At first I didn't take it serious, but he was jabbing a knife at me. The knife looked like a hunting knife about 6-7" long and 1" wide. While jabbing the knife he demanded my large bills. He repeatedly said, "Large bills, large bills, gimme your large bills".

He looked like he had dirty blonde hair, which was straight and hanging down the stocking at the back. He was about 5'10" or 5'11" tall with a thin build. He was wearing a dark greenish/mustard coloured tweed sweater with a round neck. I believed by his voice that he was about 25 years old. He had no accent.

I gathered the large bills from my bottom drawer and gave him 4 - $100.00 bills and 2 - $50.00 bills. He wasn't satisfied with that and he then shouted, "I want all of it." I then gave him $1000.00 in $20.00 bills and $250.00 in $5.00 bills. He shouted, "I want more large, more large." and I told him I didn't have any. Then he said, "I want more money." so I gave him my $20.00 bills, $10.00 bills and my "bait" money that the bank keeps the serial numbers for. The "bait" money consisted of 10 - $10.00 bills. He then turned and ran out of the bank.

Periodically while gathering my money I was looking at Wilma Samson who was two wickets to my left. The guy in front of her was pointing a gun at her. I think it was a revolver with a long barrel.

I had approximately $2,750.00 stolen from my drawers.

I did not see the man who had the gun very well and I don't remember what he looked like.

signed Barb Smith
Monday, January 10, 1994
5:20 p.m.

8

Notebook

Officers make countless observations and participate in innumerable conversations which they are expected to recall during testimony several months later. Consequently, accurate, precise memory recall without assistance is unlikely.

Notebooks facilitate memory recall. Notebook recording skills reflect an officer's habits and are directly related to the quality of testimony given in court.

Purpose: A notebook's purpose is to facilitate memory recall. The time and reason for recall varies. For example:

(i)   shortly after or within a few <u>hours</u> of an incident for the purpose of writing a G.O.R. or an arrest report. The elapsed time is not lengthy and retention maybe high but recorded notes are essential to remember all information relevant to report writing.

(ii)   a few <u>days</u> after an incident. Lengthy investigations require communication among several officers.   Effective communication is dependent upon accurate notes. Additionally, citizens' complaints require precise recall during internal investigations which may occur within days of an incident.

(iii)   several <u>months</u> after an offence. Court trials occur several months after an offence date. During the elapsed time, countless other observations are made. The combination of a time lapse with learning new information will interfere with the recall of a specific event. Although the notebook itself is not admissible, physical evidence, the observations must be introduced at a trial by means of verbal testimony, under oath. Notebooks simply assist recall during testimony.

Essentially, a notebook's purpose is to assist an officer in accurately and precisely explaining any event any time in the future without vagueness or ambiguity.

Objective: To record the chronological explanation of all actions taken during daily tours of duty, including precise, accurate records of:
- complaints investigated
- motor vehicle collisions investigated
- witnesses interviewed
- accused persons arrested and interrogated
- names, addresses, phone numbers, dates of birth of all persons with whom contact is made
- searches conducted
- physical evidence seized
- observations of offences
- relevant times of these actions

Developing notetaking skills: Notebook recording is a skill which requires written recreation of an occurrence or event. Novice note takers have a tendency to record and explain events in general terms. Note taking skill increases by explaining an event in specific, precise terms. Skill development and mastery is attained by applying principles combined with experience gained through repetition.

The following progressions may facilitate note taking and recording development:

(i)   learn **general format**
(ii)   learn **general principles**
(iii)   **apply general principles** to specific types of occurrences
   •   gain experience through daily repetition
   •   constantly identify deficient, vague notes and correct future note taking procedure by correcting the deficiencies

GENERAL FORMAT: Each police department may have a specific note taking format that officers must follow. However, it is generally accepted that all officers are required to maintain a bound, pocket-size notebook. The notebook should be constructed so that pages cannot be inserted or removed. Except for leaving a line to separate one day from the next, every line should be written on. Use a single line, drawn through an error to delete it. Do not obliterate the error or white it out; it should be readable. Initial the error.

The general format is as follows:

1. Begin each tour of duty with the date
2. Record duty hours
3. Record time reported for duty - use 24 hour clock, <u>no law prevents am/pm system however</u>
4. Note weather conditions, including road surface, ie. dry, wet, icy spots, visibility, ie. clear, rain, snow
5. Record briefing time: assembly in police station where supervisor informs officer of relevant patrol information
6. Note patrol area
7. State police vehicle number
8. Give partner's name if applicable
9. Record time the police vehicle was searched and the search results
10. Note time in service, use 10-code
11. Give time of first action: time of arrival, <u>use 10-code</u>, at the complaint dispatched to, using the address
12. State type of complaint
13. Note relevant information from GOR
14. Note time of departure, signifying your time back in service
15. Repeat in service/out of service format for all other actions and duties throughout the tour of duty
16. Note time out of service and off duty
17. Sign the notebook
18. Have your supervisor sign next

Example:

	Monday, Nov. 28, 1994
	19:00-07:00
18:23	Report for duty
	roads: wet
	visibility: clear, light snow
18:30	Briefing
	patrol area: 12-34
	vehicle: #345
	partner: Smith
18:43	Searched vehicle - negative results
18:45	10-8
18:57	10-7 10 King St.
	RE: BREAK, ENTER & THEFT
	complainant: June Weaver
	address: same
	telephone number: 555-1234
	D.O.B.: 40-01-05
	June is the owner of the house. She left for work at 08:00 07:45. She returned home at 18:45. Point of entry was the back door (describe damage and all physical evidence found and seized) stolen items:
	1. Describe each item by: type, make, model, serial number, colour and all UNIQUE identifying features)
19:43	10-8
24:00	10-43
01:00	10-8 out of service - detachment
06:45	off duty
	Officer's signature, supervisor's signature
	Tuesday, Nov. 29, 1994

GENERAL PRINCIPLES: Notebook principles are a set of rules and guidelines that act as a basis for recording notes in general. The use of the following principles is intended to eliminate vagueness and ambiguity while improving the description of an event:

1.   The most prominent principle that will dramatically improve notebook recording is to <u>avoid paraphrasing</u>. Paraphrasing refers to the use of words, terms and phrases that name an offence.
     The following terms should <u>not</u> be used when explaining or recreating an observation or incident:
   - stole/steal - "I saw the accused <u>steal</u> the car."
   - damaged - "He then <u>damaged</u> the door."
   - threatened - "He <u>threatened</u> her on several occasions."
   - assaulted - "The accused <u>assaulted</u> her after he <u>threatened</u> her."
   - break and enter - "I saw the accused <u>break and enter</u> into the house."
   - attempt/tried - "He <u>tried</u> to force the door open but the <u>attempt</u> failed."

     The use of these offence names does not describe the act. These terms are conclusions that a trial judge must make. Replace these examples of paraphrasing with the exact acts, conduct or words that constituted the offence.
     This rule applies to verbal testimony in court. Using paraphrased terms constitutes drawing a conclusion. This is reserved for the trial judge only, not the witness. Replacing the paraphrasing with an explanation of the act or words will immediately improve the quality of the notes and ultimately the credibility of the officer's testimony..

2.   Record all conversations with accused persons <u>verbatim</u>, referring to word for word direct quotes. Avoid the following examples of paraphrased conversation:
   - confessed/admitted - "During questioning, the accused <u>confessed</u> that he committed the robbery and <u>admitted</u> that he used a stolen gun."
   - consented - "The accused <u>consented</u> to have his car searched."
   - right to counsel
   - cautioned - "The accused was informed of his <u>right to counsel</u>, and he was <u>cautioned</u>. The accused <u>understood</u> both."
   - understood

     The issues represented by the above terms are conclusions for a trial judge to make, not the witness. The verbatim conversation must be recorded and stated during testimony.

3.   Record the presence or absence of factors that affect observation, including:
   (i)   intent to learn - to determine whether an awareness existed that an event or incident was about to occur, describe the circumstances that occurred immediately preceding the observation
   (ii)   the time the observation was made
   (iii) position - explain your distance relative to each observation
   (iv)   duration of the observation
   (v)   the time the notes were recorded - notes may be used to refresh memory during testimony only if they were made as soon as practicable after the observation. This record will help prove that no unreasonable delays which may prevent the use of the notebook occurred.
   (vi)   activity between time of observation and time the incident is recorded. Some time lapse usually occurs. The type of activity that occurred during this time lapse is significant. It must be determined whether excessive activity interfered with the mental repetition of the observation before recall was made and the notes written. This issue may be critical regarding the evaluation of credibility. (For further reference, see pg. 144, Criminal Investigation: McGraw-Hill Ryerson.)

4.   Thorough, accurate descriptions of an accused person should be recorded despite the capability of identifying the accused at the trial by means of facial recognition. Identification of an accused person in court is an opinion. The value of the opinion is elevated if the basis of the opinion is explained. The accused's physical stature and appearance will constitute the basis of the opinion.

5.   Physical evidence seized by an officer must be sufficiently described to make a positive identification of the item at the trial. Positive identification refers to the recognition of it and proving beyond reasonable doubt that the item introduced at the trial was the same item seized. Positive identification may be facilitated by recording:
- type of item
- make, model
- serial number
- colour
- size
- unique features exclusive to that item, including:
  - (i)   damage
  - (ii) wear marks
  - (iii) officer's initials - record the exact time the initials were written and their location on the item.

Successful positive identification will ensure the admissibility of the item at the trial. Conversely, failure to describe and identify the item may create doubt as to whether the item introduced at the trial is the same item that was seized. This could result in the exclusion of the item from the trial.

APPLY GENERAL PRINCIPLES to specific types of occurrences: The types of occurrences that require notes vary widely in nature. They include:
- complaints made by victims, i.e. criminal offences, provincial offences, motor vehicle collisions
- witness interviews
- observation of offences
- accused person/suspect interrogations

The type of notes required may be divided into two categories:
- (i)   information constituting hearsay evidence: this information will be required to write general occurrence reports, arrest reports, witness statements, and, Crown briefs. However, this information cannot be stated during the receiving officer's testimony because hearsay is generally inadmissible.
- (ii)   observations perceived by the officer's senses: this includes offences that officers find being committed. The relevant notes made are significant because observations perceived by one's own senses are admissible if they are relevant and no exclusionary rule exists.

Officers commonly do not write notes directly into an approved notebook at the time the information is received or the observations are made. Instead, (rough notes), referring to notes written informally on paper other than an approved notebook, are made. The contents are later transcribed by the officer into an approved notebook.

When should rough notes be retained? Rough notes written in relation to observations made by the officer's senses should be retained because the rough notes were the original ones made. After transcribing the contents into an approved notebook, the rough notes may be attached to the relevant pages by staple or paper clip. However, rough notes constituting hearsay evidence need not be retained after the contents are transcribed into an approved notebook.

The notes in a bound, approved notebook must never be altered in any manner. Alteration includes:
- (i)   rewriting a notebook to change original notes

(ii)   removing and inserting pages. This does not refer to the attachment of rough notes; it refers to the removal of approved notebook pages and replacing them with pages intended to resemble the original.

The following example illustrates the application of general principles to a specific occurrence.

Example:

19:10	(10-code for out of service)
	10 King St. regarding a Break, Enter and Theft.
	Complainant: Ward Clemen
hearsay	Address: same.
	Phone: 555-1234.
	D.O.B. : 40-01-20.
	Ward is the owner of the house. He left home at
	07:45 today. Returned at 19:00 hrs. Point of entry:
- observation made by own senses	back door (south side). Inside wooden door was open.
- officer may testify about this to	The door and the frame were splintered. Seven
corroborate complaint	dents were on the wooden door near the door knob.
	Nothing in the house was touched. The only item
hearsay	missing was: - 20" Sony colour T.V. set, - grey and
	black frame, - serial number A1Z345, - silver square
	volume button had been missing, - value = $500.00,
	- stolen from the living room.
19:45	10-code for in service

Recording the Interrogation: Each officer involved in the interrogation of a suspect must make personal notes in a formal notebook. The Ontario Court of Appeal, in *R. v. Barrett (1993)* stated that every officer should make *independent notes*, meaning individual notes. For example, an unsatisfactory procedure is for one officer to record the notes and the second officer to simply sign the first officers' notebook.

The precise conversation that occurs during interrogation must be recorded *verbatim*, referring to direct quotes or word-for-word. Verbatim notes undoubtedly will not be perfectly accurate; they can only reflect the officer's best attempt at recollection. The purpose of verbatim notes is to recreate the precise conversation for a *voir dire*. Silence, pauses and conduct must be included in the notes. *Rough notes* are usually made during an interrogation. These, combined with the officer's memory, will assist the writing of verbatim notes in the formal notebook. The rough notes are retained for court; they may be stapled to the respective page of the notebook or kept in a file. They should be brought to court and kept by the officer during testimony.

During an interrogation, the officer asking the questions usually is not the officer writing the rough notes. These verbatim notes, are not expected to be complete. The Ontario Court of Appeal, in *R. v. Barrett (1993)* stated that complete notes are not expected from the officer conducting the interrogation. In the *Barrett* case, the interrogating officer recorded every question and answer while the second officer merely witnessed the interrogation and took no notes. The second officer simply signed the first officer's notebook and copied the notes into his own notebook. The court noted surprise that the interrogating officer's notes not only were purported to be verbatim, but also that they were the only set in existence.

Therefore, each officer not only should make his or her own notes, the individual notes must reflect the individual officer's *own personal observations and memory*, not that of the other officer's. Some discussion between partners is inevitable and acceptable if each officer's respective notes reflect only what the individual officer can remember as being true. The most significant aspect is the officer's testimony in court. Each officer must testify only about what s/he can honestly remember, not what another officer remembered. In *Archibald v. The Queen (1956)*, the Quebec Superior Court stated that a police officer may discuss observations with another officer as long as s/he can swear under oath and testify that the personal observations are nothing but the truth.

Additionally, the officer's notes must be *contemporaneous*, meaning that they were made by the officer at the time of the observation or shortly afterward. Consequently, unreasonable delays between the interrogation and the recording of the notes may prevent the use of the notes by the officer during court.

Procedure

1. Write rough notes during an interrogation. Retain all rough notes for court by stapling them to the formal notebook or keeping them in a separate file.
2. Enter the time when the verbatim conversation was recorded in the notebook, to prove the notes were contemporaneous. Use of notes during testimony must be preceded by permission from the trial judge; this *requires proof* that the notes are contemporaneous.
3. Each officer must make independent, personal notes in a formal notebook. Therefore, one set of combined notes is insufficient and simply copying a partner's notes is inappropriate. If collaboration with a partner occurred, record this fact and *admit it* when asked, during testimony. Use rough notes and recollection to record *verbatim* conversation. Avoid paraphrasing the entire conversation or portions of it. The format of the conversation may be written by printing the person's initials followed by the verbatim statement. Examples are found the case study which follows.
4. Interrogations conducted by one officer may not have the benefit of extensive rough notes. Writing during conversation diminishes the effects of questioning and comments. Therefore, a lone officer must rely upon memory to record verbatim conversation. The interrogating officer's notes likely will not be precise and are not expected to be perfect.
5. Draw a rough diagram of the room in the formal notebook, including:
   * seating arrangement
   * doors, windows, furniture

In summary, do not write notes or testify about conversation that is not clearly remembered from one's own memory.

Example

Prelude:

On Friday, February 7, 1986, Wally was arrested for a corner store robbery committed six day earlier. The arrest was based upon reasonable grounds that were formulated from facts received from an informant. The investigators were *certain about the accused's guilt.*

The arrest occurred at the residence of Wally's girlfriend. He was cautioned and informed of his right to counsel. Wally responded, "What? I was with my girlfriend."

He was driven to a police station and was interrogated by two investigators in a spacious, contemporary office.

The verbatim conversation was recorded in a notebook as follows:

Police Officer #1: Is there any reason why you robbed the store?
Wally: "I didn't. I don't know what you're talking about."
Police Officer #1: "It's not a question of if you did it, but why you did it. Was it just for the money?"
Wally: (no response)
Police Officer #1: "There's got to be a reason for you to rob a store and grab the girl. Were you short of cash?"
Wally: "I don't know anything about this."
Police Officer #1: "Wally, we've gone through this. There's no question about it. There's got to be a reason for you to do this."
Wally: (no response)
Police Officer #1: It seems a little more serious than shoplifting. Why would you grab the girl too? Why would you do something like this?"
Wally: (held out his right hand; rubbed his thumb and fingers) "Cash."
Police Officer #1: "Are you that bad off?"
Wally: (nodded his head)
Police Officer #1: "What about welfare or something like that?"
Wally: "There's problems at my house. My dad hasn't worked for five years. What's welfare worth? You can't even go out and buy a pair of jeans."
Police Officer #1: "But at least it's something."
Wally: "But there's more to it."
Police Officer #1: "Are you working?"
Wally: "I was, just part time. I was working at some subdivision doing dry walling. I couldn't believe it the next day that I did this. I've never done anything like it before. She's not hurt bad is she?"
Police Officer #1: "No."
Wally: "But all I did was shove her away. I can't believe I did it."
Police Officer #1: "She says there's marks on her neck and that you grabbed her hair."
Wally: "I shoved her. I reached into the till and she grabbed the till or something and I shoved her down. Boy, I feel like crying right now."
Police Officer #2: "Are you going to give us a statement?"
Wally: "Sure. I've never done anything like this before. I drank a lot that day. I go to straighten out."

9

Private Policing/Security Reports

Members of private policing enforce laws by using citizens' authorities allowed by a variety of sources of law. Although citizens' authorities are limited in comparison with police officers' authorities, private police members perform similar duties and procedures as police officers, including:
- arresting offenders
- searching persons
- seizing evidence
- using force
- observing offences and relevant circumstances
- interviewing witnesses
- charging offenders
- testifying in court
- interogating suspects

Private police members are accountable for their actions in the same manner as police officers. Consequently, private police members must write notebooks and reports to justify the use of an authority and to assist in potential court testimony.

This chapter discusses the principles of private police notetaking and report writing. Examples are included.

NOTEBOOKS: The reason for maintaing a notebook is the same in private or public policing:
- record, in chronolgical order, all duties performed
- justify all authorities and procedures used during a tour of duty
- explain investigations to employers and members of the criminal justice system
- provide information to the police
- refresh memory during court testimony

The principles of notebook writing are the same for private police and public police because their is no difference between these two types of notebooks. Any observations made, or explanation of a procedure perfomed requires precision, specificity and accuracy regardless of who the author is.

Therefore, *private police notebook principles* are the same as those explained in Chapter 8. An emphasis must be made by employers and private police members to consistently use these principles to ensure the high quality of investigations and court testimony.

REPORTS: Private police members may be required to write a vaiety of reports, including:
- offence occurrence reports
- arrest reports

- response to alarms
- property checks
- strike scene reports

The documentation of an offence committed, arrest made, or procedure used has the same objective regardless if the author is a police officer or member of private policing. **A common misconception is that a police officer's reports should have greater detail than a report written by a private police member.** All law enforcement reports require the same degree of specific facts and accuracy. These reports will be read by members of the criminal justice system and by employers of private police. The quality of a written report directly reflects the character of a law enforcement officer.

Consequently, the *principles of private police reports* are the same as those explained in Chapter 2; to ensure specificity and accuracy of narrative reports.

WITNESS STATEMENTS: Witness statements may represent the most important type of report completed by private police members. A proper statement should fully explain the extent of a person's observations and actions taken, while leaving no questions or ambiguity in the reader's mind. Readers will include prosectuors, defence lawyers and police officers.

An improper statement will not only hinder the investigation and trial, it may cause the writer's reputation to suffer.

Witness statements explain observations made by a:

i) witness other than a private police member. The statement should be dictated by the witness and written by the private police member. The statement will be the result of an interview that generates sufficient facts in a structured order.

ii) private police member. The observations may include witnessing the commission of an offence, the events during an arrest, and conversation with an offender. Private police members usually write their own statement, rather than dictating the information to a police officer. Thus, private police members must develop the same skills as those used by a public police officer.

The significance of witness statements in private policing is:

i) they explain, to the prosecutor and to defence lawyers who receive the statements as part of disclosure, the anticipated testimony of the witness.

ii) they are analyzed by police officers to determine whether the circumstances reported by the witness constitutes reasonable grounds

Witness statements must reflect **only the observations perceived by the witness's senses. Hearsay evidence should not be included.** Hearsay evidence includes observations not seen or heard by the witness; another person saw or heard it and told the witness.

Additionally, witness statements should not be unstructured or vague. The observations should be explained in chronological order. General terms and paraphrasing should be avoided, and should be replaced with specific explanations.

The *principles and procedures* used to write a witness statement do not differ for public and private police. All statements must be written in the same manner. Therefore, private police members should use the principles explained in Chapter 5 to write their own or another persons' witness statement.

Summary: It has been repeatedly emphasized that public and private police reports do not differ and require the same writing principles. Private police organizations must set and consistently maintain high standards regarding the documentation of observations and occurrences. High standards in report writing skills prevents unneccessary criticism of investigations and also elevates the credibility of all enforcement personnel. Law enforcement students must never minimize the importance of report writing skills. These skills will effect the perception of others regarding the writer's competence, and career advancement.

Like any other skill, the mastery of report writing requires the study of principles, considerable practice and experience. Repeated use of the proper procedures will ensure that advanced report writing skills become a habit.

COVER PAGE: In private policing, these may be designed by individual companies. They often contain general information, similar to a police report cover page, and are usually completed by filling in blanks or checking boxes.

Example of a Cover Page

BUSINESS/COMPANY   **INCIDENT**

name:_____   nature: _____
address:_____   location: _____
phone: _____   time occurred: _____
fax: _____   time reported: _____

REPORTED BY   **WITNESSES**

name:_____   1. _____
(H)address: _____   2. _____
(H) phone: _____   3. _____
D.O.B.: _____   4. _____
(B)address:_____   5. _____
(B) phone: _____
(B) fax: _____

Description of damage (inc. value): _____
_____

Description of stolen items (inc. value): _____
_____

Injuries: _____
_____

SUBJECT/ACCUSED

name: _____   desc: HT _____   WT _____
address: _____   age _____ hair _____ eyes _____
phone: _____   clothing _____
D.O.B._____   _____

arrested by: _____   desc. of vehicle: make: _____
time of arrest:_____   model: _____ year: _____
location of arrest:_____   type: _____   colour: _____
searched: Yes (by)_____No __   features: _____
items seized:
interrogated: Yes   No
confession: Yes   No

Time police notified: _____   Time of police arrival: _____
Police officer's name: _____

                    Written by: _____

Format for General Occurrence Report (occurrence - "Theft under $5000.00)

> The Company is a business premises situated at **(address)**. It **(state business function, i.e. produces, manufactures etc.)** The premises are composed of **(describe building(s) and property, e.g. number of buildings, floors etc.).**
>
> On **(date)**, The Company was open between the hours of **(specific times)**. During that time, **(describe relevant activity that occurred, e.g. open for business, employees were working).**
>
> **(Describe items)** were stored/situated in **(specify location)**. The items were described as **(general description and specific description, value).** They were last seen by **(name)** at **(time)**, or **(explain how the presence of the items were accounted for, before the theft occurrred).**
>
> At **(time)**, **(name of person)** discovered that the following items were missing **(if same, state "the items mentioned above")** or **(specify which of the above items were missing).**
>
> **(Describe the appearance of the crime scene with specific attentionto potential physical evidence, i.e. items touched where fingerprints may be located, , shoeprints found).**
>
> The following employees worked during that shift: **(name, address, phone, date of birth).** **(Witness's name)** was interviewed by **(security personnel)** at **(location).** He/she reported the following: **(specific observations).**
>
> Repeat for each witness or employee. Explain all other relevant observations or information.
>
> At **(time)**, **(name of person, agency, police)** was notified.

Example #1 - Arrest Report: Theft under $5,000.00.

> This charge arises from an incident which occurred on May 27, 1996, at 11:00 a.m., at The Store, situated at 1234 First Street in St. Catharines, Ontario.
>
> The accused person in this matter is Eddie Harkins, D.O.B. Jan. 15, 1970. He lives at 4321 Second St., Hamilton, Ontario.
>
> On Monday, May 27, 1996, The Store opened for business at 10:00 a.m. At 10:59 a.m., Harkins entered the store alone. He walked down several aisles, looked at various items but selected nothing.
>
> At 11:00 a.m., Harkins entered the men's clothing department. He selected a plain black sweatshirt from a shelf and concealed the sweatshirt inside a jacket that he was wearing. The sweatshirt is described as: black, long sleeve, size large, a collar tag with "The Sweatshirt Company" printed on it. The sweatshirt is valued at $39.95. A price tag is attached to the right sleeve.
>
> Harkins walked toward the front of The Store. He passed the cash registers. He did not pay for the item and left The Store via the front entrance.
>
> June Brunett, retail investigator, witnessed the entire incident and followed Harkins without losing sight of him. She apprehended Harkins on the sidewalk in front of The Store. She arrested him for "Theft under $5,000.00," informed him of the right to counsel and cautioned him. Eddie was escorted to the security office. He voluntarily gave the sweatshirt to June Brunett, who seized it.
>
> The police were called at 11:05 a.m. Cst. Friendly arrived at 11:09 a.m. and took custody of Harkins, arrested him for "Theft under $5,000.00," informed him of the right to counsel, and cautioned him. Cst. Friendly seized the sweatshirt. The officer released Harkins at 11:30 a.m. by means of an appearance notice.

Example #2 - Witness Statement: Theft under $5,000.00

June Brunett will say: (or, "Anticipated evidence of June Brunett"):

I am thirty-eight years old. I am employed by The Store, situated at 1234 First Street, in the City of St. Catharines, where I hold the position of retail investigator.

On Monday, May 27, 1996, I was working the 10 a.m. - 6 p.m. shift, assigned to internal patrol. I wore street clothes, not a uniform. At 10:57 a.m., I was standing in an aisle near the front entrance. I saw a man enter The Store alone, via the front entrance. He was later identified as Eddie Harkins. He wore a jacket that was opened.

I saw Harkins walk down four aisles. He looked at various items but selected nothing. I followed him at a distance of about twenty feet.

At 11:00 a.m., I saw Harkins enter the men's clothing department. He stopped at a shelf where sweatshirts were located. I was standing in the next aisle, about twenty feet from him. I had an unobstructed view of the front of Harkins.

I saw Harkins select a black sweatshirt. He place it inside his jacket. He walked toward the front of the store. I followed him at a distance of about twenty feet. Harkins walked past the cash register. He did not stop and he did not pay for the sweatshirt.

Harkins left The Store via the front entrance. I ran to him and apprehended him on the sidewalk in front of The Store. I had not lost sight of him from the time I saw him place the sweatshirt in his jacket until I apprehended him.

I took hold of his right arm and he stopped walking. I said to him, "My name is June Brunett. I am a retail investigator at The Store. You're under arrest for stealing the sweatshirt."

Harkins removed the sweatshirt from inside the jacket and said, "Here it is. I didn't think anyone saw me steal it." He gave me the sweatshirt and I seized it. I read him the right to counsel by saying, "(insert verbatim, the words used). Do you understand?" Harkins replied, "Yes."

I then read the caution to him by saying, "(insert the words used verbatim). Do you understand?" Harkins answered, "Yes."

I told Harkins, "You have to come with me to the retail investigator's office." Harkins said, "OK" and accompanied me. We arrived at the office at 11:05 a.m. I phoned the police at that time.

I examined the sweatshirt. It is described as: black in colour, long sleeve, size large, collar tag with "The Sweatshirt Company" printed on it, and a price tag attached to the right sleeve with $39.95 printed on the tag. I initialed the price tag.

I asked Harkins questions to obtain his personal information to write an arrest report.

Cst. Friendly arrived at 11:09 a.m. I informed the officer about my observations. Cst. Friendly arrested Harkins for "Theft under $5,000.00," informed him of the right to counsel and cautioned him. Harkins stated that he understood all the information.

I gave the sweatshirt to Cst. Friendly. I saw Cst. Friendly initial the price tag.

At 11:30 a.m., Cst. Friendly served Harkins an appearance notice and released him from custody.

Example #3 - Arrest Report: Mischief under $5,000.00

This charge arises from an incident which occurred on May 28, 1996, at 10:00 p.m., in the front lobby of an apartment building situated at 9876 Third Street, _____, Ontario. The apartment building is privately policed by the _____ Housing Authority.

The accused person in this matter is Wally Clement, D.O.B. May 1, 1973. He lives at 5432 Fourth St., _____, Ontario.

At 10:00 p.m., Clement entered the lobby of the apartment building. He was intoxicated at the time. Micheal DiLorenzoni and Whitey Harrison, apartment tenants, were in the lobby, waiting for their ride to arrive.

Clement banged on the interior locked glass door, shouting, "Let me in" and shouted profanities. He repeated banging on the door and shouting obscenities. Two tenants from the first floor opened their apartment doors and told Clement to be quiet.

DiLorenzoni called the Housing Authority private police from a telephone in the lobby. Eddie Artelle, a private police member, responded to the call and arrived in the lobby at 10:01 p.m. He saw Clement banging on the glass door with his fist and heard Clement shouting, "Let me in," adding several obscenities. Clement kicked the door causing the glass to shatter.

Artelle arrested Clement for "Mischief under $5,000.00," informed him of the right to counsel and cautioned him. Artelle escorted Clement to the security office. The police were called at 10:03 p.m. Cst. Friendly arrived at 10:06 p.m. took custody of Clement, arrested him for "Mischief under $5000.00," informed him of the right to counsel, cautioned him and transported him to the police station.

Clement was later released by means of a promise to appear. The damaged door was later repaired at a cost of $750.00.

Example #4 - Witness Statement: Mischief under $5,000.00

I am thirty years old. I am a member of the _____ Housing Authority, where I hold the position of private security guard. I am assigned to patrol an apartment complex, situated at 9876 Third St., _____, Ontario.

On Tuesday, May 28, 1996, I was working the 7p.m. - 7a.m. shift at 9876 Third St., _____, Ontario. At 10:00 p.m., I was in the security office. I received information from a phone call. As a result, I attended at the lobby, arriving there at 10:01 p.m.

Three people were in the lobby: Wally Clement, the accused person; Micheal DiLorenzoni and Whitey Harrison. Two tenants on the first floor were standing in the hallway.

A locked, glass door is situated inside the lobby, separating the lobby from the remainder of the apartment building. I saw Clement banging on the glass door, with a clenched fist shouting, "Let me in, (insert verbatim obscene language)." I walked toward Clement. He repeated banging on the glass door with his fist and shouted again, "Let me in, (verbatim obscene language)."

As I approched Clement, I smelled an alcoholic beverage on his breath, I saw that his eyes were bloodshot and he staggered when he stood banging on the door. His speech was slurred. I saw Clement kick the door with his right foot. The glass shattered.

I was wearing a uniform that had a shoulder patch with _____ Housing Authority printed on it. I took hold of Clement's arm and said, "You're under arrest for "Mischief under $5000.00. We're going to the security office. Stop screaming. You're disturbing people."

I then informed Clement of his right to counsel by saying, "(insert verbatim the words used). Do you understand?" Clement answered, "Yes." I then cautioned him by saying, "(insert verbatim the words used). Do you understand?" Clement answered, "Yes."

I searched Clement for weapons. No items were found. I then said, "Come with me." Clement stated, "Sorry for breaking the door. I was mad and I had to see somebody. I think I've had too much to drink."

I escorted Clement to the security office. I telephoned the police at 10:03 p.m. Cst. Friendly arrrived at 10:06 p.m. I informed Cst. Friendly about my observations and the officer took custody of Clement.

I heard Cst. Friendly tell Clement that he was under arrest for "Mischief under $5,000.00." He told him his right to counsel and the caution. Cst. Friendly asked if he understood at the end of each instruction. Clement answered, "yes" to each.

Cst. Friendly escorted Clement to a police vehicle which was parked in front of the security office. Clement entered the back seat of the police vehicle. Clement cooperated throughout the arrest.

Appendix

Glossary of common terms

actus reus: the physical act of an offence
mens rea: the mental element of an offence; the intent to commit an offence
criminal responsibility: the combination of "actus reus" and "mens rea"
facts in issue: the elements that compose an offence
prima facie case: case where all the "facts in issue" have been proven beyond reasonable doubt
verbatim: word-for-word direct quote

Words commonly used in Law Enforcement Report Writing

absence	beligerent	circumstantial	deceive	evidentiary
accelerate		committal	deception	existence
accomplice		compel	deliberate	exited
admissible		complainant	demerit	extradition
advantageous		compulsory	dual procedure	
assault		conspiracy		
attendance				
autopsy				
auxiliary				
fulfill	harass	indictable	jurisdiction	licence
fictitious	hearsay	inebriated		
		intentionally		
		interrogation		
maintained	nunchakus	obscenities	physician	recognizance
maintenance		occasion	possession	relevant
mandatory		occurrence	post-mortem	repetition
		offence	principal	retaliation
			principle	
			privilege	
			proximity	
			psychiatrist	
			psychological	
separate		territorial	vicinity	withhold
sergeant		traveled		
sobriety		trespass		
spontaneously				
summary conviction				
supplementary				
superintendent				
symptoms				

Notes

Notes

Notes

Notes

Notes

Notes